Dear Dad,
I Broke the Cycle:
A Grown Woman's
Guide
to
Getting over
an
Absentee Father

www.ikeshiacapre.com
Cover Design by Nnenna Lovette. Graphic & Web
Design Services

Edited by Val Pugh-Love
ISBN 978-0-9966247-0-1

Acknowledgments

First and foremost, I want to **thank God** for giving me this vision. He gave me the courage to be vulnerable for my readers. I believe He wanted me to write this book to let other fatherless women know that they are not alone. Moreover, He wants me to assure women that they do not have to be a product of their environment.

Secondly, I would like to **thank all the men who used me**. I was hurt and lost, but now I can say that I am restored and ready to move on with my life. Without you, I wouldn't be where I am today, nor would I have a juicy story to tell LOL.

Next, I want to **thank the Miller/Redd family**. I tell you all the time that I wouldn't be the woman I am today without you all. I hope that I make you proud by "broadening my horizons" and by letting you see who I really am. Your support and guidance made me believe that I could do anything, and for that I am grateful.

Also, I want to **thank all of my friends**. I know most of you might have thought I was crazy when I first introduced the idea of writing a book. Nevertheless, without your support, I couldn't have possibly made this happen.

Of course, I want to **thank my family** for supporting with me on this journey. I appreciate your encouragement, and I thank you for being my cheerleaders when I didn't think I was going to make it.

To anyone else reading this book, **thank you** for getting to know my background and myself. I hope that I have helped you in some way. If I have not, I pray someone is placed in your life to help you get on the right path and fulfill your purpose in life.

~ Ikeshia Capre

Contents

Foreword

This book is dedicated to all the fatherless women across the world. I hope my story motivates and ensures you that you are not alone. We have all made mistakes and that is natural. However, I encourage you to stay focused and believe God has a plan for your life.

Ikeshia Capre

Letter to My Father

Dear Dad,

When you read this, I hope I don't disappoint you. Your "princess" that you attempted to contact not even once a year has many flaws, but hopefully you will still see me as your princess. I wish I could take back all my thoughtless decisions and reach out to you in my most desperate and vulnerable moments, but that wasn't an option. With you being addicted to drugs, being in and out of jail, and making bastard children, I felt lost and lonely. I had no choice but to figure things out on my own, and my failed attempts were countless. The men I sought love from couldn't possibly have given me the love that you should have given. All I've ever received from a man is lust. Nothing more, nothing less.

My self-worth was so low that I should have turned into a corpse, because my soul was dead. So dead, that I felt my life was no longer valuable. The pain and suffering you put Mother and me through, both emotionally and financially shaped us into the women we are today. Each time my mother couldn't pay a bill or when her car broke down and she couldn't afford to fix it, I grew angry at you. When she couldn't afford to give us a Christmas and we had to sign up for charity, I grew angrier at you. Unfortunately, I was angry at her as well. I would cry out every night when I saw the hurt in Mother's eyes caused by your failure to be a father. Since my mother chose to stay supportive in your darkest moments, it is because of you that her life became less valuable each time you came back.

When I needed you the most, I didn't have a reliable source to contact, because you were always on the move. Every time I went to school or started a new job, people would ask what my parents did for a living. When it came to you, I remained silent and embarrassed for your lack of effort to be a father. I always felt that since I was your first born, I should have been your first priority, but I wasn't. Because I was so conditioned to this treatment, the

*decisions I made and the men I allowed in my life made me
hate myself.*

*I want you to know that I speak from honesty and
truth. I will reveal my bare moments in the rawest form. I
will introduce you to my world that you never knew existed.
This will hurt you. You will become ashamed of not only
being an absent father, but to know your oldest child was
stripped of her character by every man she created a soul
tie with throughout her life. Although this may be one of the
deepest cuts you will experience, I learned over time to
bounce back and make sure my life was the opposite of
yours.*

Signed,

Your Little Princess

Chapter One – Rainbow Bright

It was Sunday morning, and the church was lit up with sunlight and gospel voices blaring through the red stained windows. My turquoise turtleneck and black skirt laid tight to my fifth grade body like a condom on males' genitals. My course hair was combed back into a black scrunch with a big bang that was curled loosely. My mother and I sat on the second row of the church in our regular Sunday seats. I guess she thought that if we sat closer to the front, we would be near the front of the line when God started handing out blessings.

I smiled my biggest smile when one of the church members came over to me and said in an exaggerated, high-pitched voice, "Heyy, Rainbow Bright! You have one of the prettiest and brightest smiles. Where are all those colorful beads Sister Brenda always puts in your hair?"

At that age, I never talked because I was extremely shy. So, I simply smiled back with no reply. The nice lady didn't attempt any additional conversation with me. Instead, she pinched my cheeks as if I were a little baby, before she hurried to her seat to prepare for offering.

When it came to offering time, my family didn't have much to give. We always had car problems, but Grandma managed to give Mother a ride to work and church until it was fixed. We lived off a nurse's aide paycheck, and my mother always seemed to make ends meet. I felt happy at the time, because the word "struggle" wasn't in my vocabulary, nor did I know the definition of it. Mother never showed that we were struggling either. In the late 90s, nurse's aide paychecks must have been manageable to feed a family and pay bills. *Dad, even though we were happy at the time, Mother never really talked much about you to me. I would only hear her talk with other adults about how you would be thrown under the jail if you denied me in court. I never knew what that meant, but it sounded bad for you.*

As the organist who wore a big hat that matched her Sunday's best and sported fingernails as long as a nail clipper sat at the front of the church and played the upbeat offering music, I noticed this boy stand up and walk to the offering table where he put $5.00 in the pan. He was my age, handsome, and wore thick gray glasses. Every time he moved, whether it was to go to the bathroom, or to get a church fan or Sunday's program for his grandmother, I could feel my heart beat fast. It was my first time feeling infatuated with someone. In my mind, I was in love. However, I clearly didn't know what love was, since the two people who were supposed to demonstrate it for me failed miserably. So, based on how I felt at that moment, he was the definition of love, and I wanted every piece of it. When he sat back down with his grandmother who had curly gray hair and glasses similar to the ones he was wearing, he turned around in the pew and looked at me. I looked down and moment was over.

After church was my favorite part. Although a nurse's aide paycheck paid the bills, extracurricular activities were not included on the list. All week I would try to snatch up any loose change that equaled a dollar to buy Sister B's cookies after church. The peanut butter and sugar cookies were inexplicably delicious. They were soft, moist, and just enough to satisfy your sweet tooth. Since so many people rushed to get in line, we had to buy the cookies in the basement of the church. There wasn't enough room upstairs in the hallway for Sister B to set up her cookie stand, according to what was read during the church announcements. The elders had complained that the line was blocking them from getting outside to their station wagons and the church van.

Just as I did every Sunday after church, I rushed downstairs to line up for my weekly dose of cookie heaven. This time, however, I was hoping I would run into the boy with the thick gray glasses downstairs. To my luck, I did. We still didn't say anything to each other. We just stared at one another for a long time. Suddenly, his grandmother grabbed his arm and called out, "Come on now." Our mutual trance was immediately interrupted as he disappeared through the doors with his grandmother. The moment, or should I say, *my moment*, was over again - at least for now.

As I was leaving the line after getting Sister B's cookies, I turned around to notice two other boys standing close to my backside. One was high-yellow and normally played the drums. He was so attractive to be so young. He had crooked teeth, but it didn't take away from his great facial features. He almost looked Mexican or Native American. His mother was a unique character. She had deep slanted eyes that almost looked as though she had a Chinese heritage. I could tell that she never shaved her legs, because I could see her leg hair through her panty hose.

Shaving was something I never indulged in, because all my life I was told, "That's a white people thing." I was too young anyway, so that wasn't on my priority list as a nine year old. His mom's legs were the least bit attractive, but her overbearing personality made up for it. He had an older sister whose hair I envied for some reason. It was always done up in these fabulous hairdos that Mother couldn't afford. I vowed to myself that when I got a job, I would always keep my hair done like that. It had to get that long first. Unfortunately, I got my first perm a year before, so my hair was the definition of stressed.

The other boy was brown-skinned and very attractive as well. He always had on the newest trend of clothing. Every time he smiled, his perfectly lined up teeth seemed to sparkle. I was always envious of people with straight white teeth, because my top row of teeth was quite odd. I had two front teeth that were perfect, and then I had one odd tooth that sat higher than the others. It never bothered me enough to ask Mother for braces, but whenever I saw straight teeth, it reminded me that I should have asked for some. His mother was a brown-skinned, big-boned lady who had marital issues with a man who looked twenty years her senior. Her husband would be at church for a few weeks straight, and then she would show up to Sunday's service alone. I just figured that he must be out in the streets, and keeping his attention on his wife was not a top priority, because the drug or other female was enough to keep him satisfied.

I could tell by the look in the boys' eyes that puberty was coming, and I wasn't going to be able to stop them from lusting after me. I saw my naked body in their brown pupils. They grinned, and I smiled back. I knew what they wanted. The brown-skinned boy grabbed my butt, and the high-yellow one laughed. It startled me, but I didn't stop him. They both started laughing and ran upstairs, and I stood there and waited for my cookies. Some days I wondered why the boys even paid me any attention. I mean, we couldn't afford fancy clothes, and my hair wasn't long. My skin was dark and sometimes ashy when Mother ran out of lotion and couldn't afford to buy more. I'm not even sure how I felt about those boys grabbing my butt. I continued to think about it as I stood in the long line, and even after we left the church.

Every Sunday after church, Mother and I always went to my grandma's house. I had a lot of cousins, but I was the one of the oldest granddaughters. My sister was just born, and my other girl cousin was only two. My nine-year old frame of mind had no time for a four-month old and a two-year old, so interactions were limited. I hung out with my boy cousins a lot. Unfortunately, they were no different from the brown-skinned and high-yellow boys at church. I was close to one boy cousin in particular. We were around the same age, so we did almost everything together. One night, Mother had to work a midnight shift at the nursing home, so I had to spend the night with my grandma. At the time, my grandma had custody of my cousin, so he lived with her. Our other girl cousin, who was my grandmother's niece, also stayed the night, because her Mother worked midnights at a nursing home as well. Since my grandmother stayed in a two bedroom apartment, all three of us had to sleep in the bed together. No biggie right? Wrong.

When we would laugh, my grandmother would yell from the other room saying, "Don't make me come in that room with the belt!" We thought our grandma was the funniest person on Earth. She wore a platinum blonde weave and was often referred to as Mary J. Blige, since her first name was Mary. We knew she wouldn't come in the room, so we quietly laughed until we fell asleep one by one. My girl cousin ended up falling asleep first. I swear that girl could snore the paint off the walls. She was twice my size and had this super thick, long, coarse hair. She wore thick glasses and had gapped teeth. She looked nothing like her mother, and I never knew who her father was. Her story seemed similar to mine. When she came around all the cousins, we'd all think she was awkward, but accepted her nonetheless, because she was blood.

This one night in particular went different from other nights that we all stayed together at my grandmother's house. At some point, I ended up at the foot of the bed, because there wasn't enough room for all three of us to lay side by side. The pajamas I had on were made of thick cotton that literally made me sweat. Not to mention, my grandma put plastic on every piece of furniture she owned, including the mattresses. When the fitted sheet slid off the mattress, getting it back on with lifeless bodies lying on it was impossible.

As I laid at the end of the bed, I struggled to go to sleep for some reason. I kept tossing and turning, and as I tried to get comfortable, things took a turn. I felt a foot between my legs. I knew it wasn't my girl cousin's foot, because her snore was hard to block out from a mile away. The foot pressed and rub against my *middle area,* and I felt this tingling sensation. Since my girl cousin was asleep, it could only be one person rubbing against me. I laid there and continued to let the foot rub up against me aggressively. At the time, I didn't know what masturbation was, but for whatever reason, I didn't make him stop. The only thing I did know was that I could never tell a soul, because we were family. Family over everything.

****

It was my last year as an elementary student, and I excelled in all subjects. Gym and Spelling were my favorite. Kids would always pick me to be on their team, because I could run fast. I'm not so sure why I loved Spelling, but if someone gave me a word, I could spell it after reviewing it a few times. I was so good at it that I went to the district spelling bee my seventh grade year. Even though I excelled in elementary school and received all kinds of awards for my hard work, my father still never came to visit me. I only recall him visiting Mother's home one night in particular. I remember both of my parents being in the back room with the lights off. When they came out, Mother was wrapped in a sheet. My father zipped up his pants and then left. I never saw him again until my eighth grade year. I assumed that my sister was conceived that night, because Mother broke the news to grandma two months later that she was pregnant.

I remember the day Mother came home with my sister. I got pushed on the playground at school and slipped on piece of ice during recess that day. I later learned that I hit my head when I fell. This explains why I was unconscious when the playground aide picked me up. She walked me to the nurse's office, and I vomited. I couldn't keep my head up, nor could I stay awake. I didn't know what was wrong. I just knew I wanted to get home. My principal drove me home and walked me inside where Mother was sitting on the couch holding my sister. He told Mother what happened and suggested that I go to the hospital. When I sat down on the couch beside her, I looked at the second seed my father created and knew she would go through life just as I did. Without a father.

Chapter 2 – Dark Girl

It was my first day of middle school, and I didn't know our new bus driver like I knew our elementary bus driver. My elementary bus driver was a cool black lady, but I knew not to cross her. She gave one strike, and you were out. She would literally stop the bus if a kid misbehaved. From that moment, we knew that whichever kid made her stop that bus was in trouble. My middle school driver had two missions. The first mission was to get the students from home to school, and the second mission was to get the students from school back home. I caught the same bus every day in the same location with the same kids. Each time the bus came, I scurried to the back with my neighborhood friends. I knew the neighborhood kids well. Very well.

One of the girls I played with had dirty blonde hair, and her mother walked her to the bus stop every day. Her mother who chained smoked and drunk a few beers a night reminded me of a trailer park resident. She had a frail body that revealed her chest bones, and you could hear the smoker's cough in her throat when she laughed or talked. Her mother's hair was very thick and dark brown, and she hardly wore her hair down. It was always parted down the middle pulled back in a ponytail. Her father worked as a mechanic. He had piercing blue eyes, and his face almost looked angelic. His hair was parted on the side and styled in a curly comb over. I rarely saw him in street clothing. He always had on his uniform, which was a navy blue coverall jumper that had permanent dirt, motor oil, and dust stains. Her older brother was tan and handsome. He had perfectly straight teeth, and almost looked as though he was Mexican. He was in high school, and he was such an outcast in the family. He was always in trouble and had different girlfriends.

One night while I was having a sleepover with his sister, his girlfriend showed up and barged into his room.

At first, I could hear them speaking in regular inside voices.

Then, I suddenly heard the girlfriend scream, "YOU CHEATED ON ME!!"

Her outburst was followed by the sound of keys as they hit against the wall, before she ran out of the house crying. His sister and I were unbothered by this event, because if it wasn't his girlfriend yelling at him, it was their parents. I would spend countless nights in their home. We took baths together, ate dinner together, and slept in the same bed. I don't know why I was there so much. I don't know if I liked the fact that they were a two-parent family home, or the fact that they could afford to buy their food instead of using the welfare paper dollars. Maybe it was because they never had to worry about their car being broken down or their electricity being disconnected. If they did have these problems, they had great poker faces. I never wanted to go home, and they treated me as their own.

The freckled face boy with the blue eyes came out onto his porch and walked ten steps to the bus stop. He had a comb over, too. He had eight other siblings with a mixture of brothers and sisters. His parents obviously didn't believe in birth control. His mother drove a minivan and had a wandering eye. It was seldom that I saw his family. His father worked a lot while the mother stayed home. They seemed nice, I guess. He was a really nice kid until he walked me home one day. It was odd behavior, because his house was right at the bus stop. I didn't know his intentions, but I let him walk me home anyway. I kind of knew what he was up to, but I didn't ask.

Since Mother had switched to retail and no longer worked midnights at the nursing home, she didn't get off until four o'clock in the afternoon. She no longer needed my grandma to babysit me, because she would be free to pick me up once she got off. I unlocked the door and sat my book bag on our rusty brown flowered couch. I made him wait in the hallway. When I came back out, he pulled me close to him. I attempted to push him off, because I felt awkward since this was not his personality, so I thought. Since I wasn't aggressive enough and too shy to tell him to stop, thankfully he only rubbed my breasts through my clothes. When he pressed up against me, I could feel this hard object in his pants. I didn't touch it. The moment only lasted a few minutes, because he left and went home once he was done. I went back into the house and turned on the TV until Mother arrived.

The other boy who stood at the bus stop with us had extremely thick dark hair and brown eyes. Comb overs must have been in style, because he had one, too. His mother and father were particularly quiet. They were very nice though, to me at least. He also had a much older brother that I didn't see much. Since the blonde-haired girl and freckled boy lived right at the bus stop, the dark haired boy and I had to walk home together. His house was white and green. I could see his driveway from my bedroom window. I would always go over to his house to play basketball on the hoop that was attached to their garage. While I was shooting around, I thought to myself, *hopefully, we will live in a house one day.*

His mother would always come out and give me the ball. He would never come out and play with me, because he had other things in mind. Almost every day after school, he would tell me to come back outside. I knew what he wanted, so I would do as I was told. Fully clothed, he would put his hand under my shirt and caress my ping pong ball sized breasts. Then, he would lie on top of me, while I laid under a prickly bush right outside my bedroom window. He would rub up against me. Hard. Dry hump me. I didn't like it, but I cooperated anyway. I tried to refuse once, but he grew angry with me. I didn't like it when people yelled or got angry with me. My feelings would be hurt, and I would cry at the drop of a dime if they did. I didn't want any trouble, so I never tried to refuse again. At the end, I was always told that I was never to tell anyone about us, because he wouldn't be my friend. This went on for two years.

At one point, he had a girlfriend. Eventually, rubbing my breasts upgraded to sucking my breasts. Although it felt good, I knew it was wrong, yet I couldn't tell anyone. Mother was always at work, so we never got caught. His parents would never ask where he was either. The moment lasted no more than five to ten minutes. His mother ended up dying our eighth grade year, and that's when it stopped. I attended the funeral, and I can remember being so upset. Not only because she was the one of the sweetest lady I knew, but also because she had no clue that her son was molesting their next door neighbor. His father got remarried to his one of his best friend's mother. Although we didn't talk much after the death of his mother, rumors spread around that he wasn't happy about his father's new marriage.

Besides having to be groped against my will every day, adjusting to middle school was tough. Extremely tough. I was no longer the teacher's favorite. I barely passed academically. Since my mother switched jobs, we were at the bottom of the totem pole when it came to finances. Our electricity was getting disconnected every other month, and welfare assistance was becoming more of a permanent crutch. Mother couldn't buy me the cool clothes that all the other kids wore, which was a big NO-NO in middle school.

I knew I was different from the other kids, and my appearance gave the first red flag. I struggled with hygiene, too. I started my menstrual cycle near the end of my fifth grade year just when the financial burden grew bigger on my mother. Pads were not cheap. There were times when Mother was too poor to even afford deodorant. If I had no pads or deodorant at the same time, Jesus himself couldn't save me from the torment that I endured at school. In addition to that, I struggled to fit in, because my hair was nappy and my skin was black. I wasn't hip to weave back then, just braids. Makeup was non-existent in our home, so the chances of trying to lighten my skin was slim to none. This lead to me being teased, bullied, and hurt.

On top of not fitting in with the kids at school, I went on my first camping trip where the other school kids were invited. I didn't know the first thing about camping, taking care of my hair, and making sure I had the right clothes and proper shoes for this type of trip. Mother and I had little knowledge when it came to these types of events. I kept myself in a shell on this trip. I didn't know the kids from the other schools, and my shyness wasn't going to allow me to try to get to know anyone. Those kids who didn't bully me from my own school were off making new friends. As much as I hated being at home, I couldn't wait to get back. Camping wasn't for me.

Finding out you don't fit in with all the other sixth grade campers socially is one thing, but it's another thing when your body doesn't agree either. A few days after we returned from the campsite, I noticed that my breathing was different. I could hear myself wheezing, but I shook it off as a cold. As the days went on, it became more and more difficult for me to breathe. After the third day, I raised my hand while sitting in Math class and asked my teacher if I could leave early, because I couldn't breathe. My teacher who had a blonde bob with a similar build to Mother, including a big butt, allowed me to go to the office to call my mother. At this point, I was wiggling around in my chair, because the loss of air in the lungs causes people to lose all train of thought. I was gasping for air, and my stomach began to cramp. Mother came to get me and took me to the hospital. Thank God she had gas in the car, or else I wouldn't be alive to tell this story.

After careful observation, the doctor told my mother that I was having an asthma attack over the course of the three days that I couldn't breathe. According to the doctor, I had bloodshot eyes from struggling to breathe for so long. He hooked me up to a machine that had a mask that strapped around my head to restore my breathing. There was a little plastic container at the bottom of the mask with a long tube that connected to the machine. He squeezed medicine into the mask's container. I now know that it was a nebulizer that would help turn the medicine into vapor to expedite it being inhaled into my lungs. He told Mother that I would have to carry an inhaler in case I suffered another asthma attack. Thank God for Medicaid, because I got my inhalers for free.

Even after Mother's superhero act, my hatred for her still came on strong, and the desire for my father to be present dwindled. Every emotion I felt remained bottled up inside, and I told no one how I felt. Everything and everyone was so different compared to elementary school. There was no division or difference, but the game just changed in junior high, and neither Mother nor I was prepared for those changes. As time went on, I no longer saw Mother's smile. I became more distant. I couldn't concentrate on anything but survival, so I went back to what I knew best. Boys.

This time, the guy of interest was one that I knew from elementary school. We were in Mrs. B's third grade class together, but I didn't notice him then. His mother and father were really sweet. His mother had a high-pitch soft voice, and I rarely saw his father. He had a younger brother who looked similar to him but quite different. We developed a friendship, and I began to start to have feelings. He asked me to be his girlfriend, and I readily accepted. We never saw each other outside of school, but one day I manage to tell him that he could come over. I was always home from school a few hours before Mother was off work, so I knew there would be plenty of time for him to come over and hang out.

He walked to my apartment, which was a bit of a walk for a sixth grader. He came inside, and we had a small conversation at first. We began to slowly peck each other on the lips, and then I slide my hands down to his middle area. He didn't stop me. I wasn't sure why I wasn't scared, but I pressed forward and unzipped his pants and placed my hands inside. He had no hair, which at that age, I didn't know there was supposed to be any. I pulled his most precious gift out and paused before I did the unthinkable. I closed my eyes and leaned down, slowly placing my mouth on the tip. I slid up and down a few times, and at one point, I was able to look up and see his eyes were closed as well. It lasted three to five minutes. There was no burst of seeds at the end, so once I lifted my head, we talked for a few before he went home. I wondered if he would tell anyone at school the next day.

The next day came, and for whatever reason, I felt that I had accomplished something. I wasn't sure why. Maybe I thought I'd look cool to the other kids. Unfortunately, the rumor of what happened between us was only hype for a short period of time. Then, I was back to being the odd man out again. I needed something else to get my mind off my foolish act, so I put my one and only talent to use. Running. I started looking for sports that would allow me to use my talent to run off some of the steam that was taking over my young thoughts.

In my seventh grade year, I wanted to be a basketball player, but my coordination to dribble a ball and run at the same time didn't mix. I was only average at playing basketball. I was able to put the ball in the hoop, but I was better at beating everyone down the court. My running ability saved me, and I made the team because of it. I didn't care which skill got me on the team, as long as it gave me some time away from home. Mother was steadily getting on my nerves with barely being able to pay her bills. She constantly struggled with putting gas in the car or having extra cash for miscellaneous items, in addition to having my little sister around who couldn't fend for herself. At least with basketball, I could release some stress and concentrate on winning, since I failed at everything else in life. When I was at basketball functions, I didn't have to think about anything. I could laugh and hangout with my teammates and secretly wish I had their life. Although I was able to break out of my shyness when I was with my teammates, my self-esteem was at rock bottom.

I resented my mother for a lot of things. I knew she was taking care of my sister and me to the best of her ability, but it wasn't enough. We needed our father. When she could afford gas money, she did attend a few of my games. I sometimes was embarrassed, because I knew she didn't drive the fanciest car, nor did she have the makeup and loving husband as all my other teammates' mothers did, but she showed up anyway. I wish my father could have been there to witness me scoring points and beating everyone down the court. The coach loved that. I loved it. Mother loved it.

Despite my father's absences, my eighth grade year was a little better. I finally had middle school all figured out. I played another year of basketball and added track and field this time. I thought to myself that if I can beat everyone on the court, I wonder what I can do on the track. Once I started winning in track, I began to gain more friends. I was feeling pretty good about myself. I was feeling so good that I thought I could say cuss words to my music teacher. Everyone in the school knew I was quiet and shy, so when I busted out with this "I'm the shit" star athlete attitude, she was shocked at my behavior. The forwardness of my new personality was a fail and got me extra laps at basketball practice. I was so embarrassed that I apologized and never did it again.

My grades were improving as well as my so-called love life. Since my first sexual encounter in sixth grade, I vowed to myself that I would never do that again, and I would actually be with a guy who liked me. This time, my guy was this super skinny boy with pale skin who had high school dropout written all over his forehead. He was not liked by many students, and the teachers cringed every time he walked into the classroom. His family told him that he would amount to nothing, and he was always sent to in-school and out of school suspensions. No one believed in him, but I did.

Whenever I was in music class, we would sneak into the hallway that connected my classroom with his classroom. He would touch me and feel on my booty. For once, I felt that he was doing it because he liked me. I would never feel on him. One day while my best friend and I were in music class, we came up with a plan to get my boy and her boy in the hallway so we could make out. We indeed succeeded. When we kissed, I could imagine hearts all around us.

I was so caught up into him that there was nothing I wouldn't do to see him. Every time he got sent to in-school suspension, I made up an excuse to go to the office to see him. We wrote notes back and forth, and one day he showed up to school with a surprise. He brought me a single rose. This was the first gift I had ever received from any male. It had a distinct scent that I still remember to this day. I kept the rose for a long time. I never wanted to get rid of it, because it was so dear to my heart.

Even after we parted ways, I would often smell the rose, and it would still smell the same. During our last few days as eighth graders, he wrote me a note stating that although we had broken up, he still cared about me. He also said that we could have sex if I wanted to do so. However, we never did until we were adults. I saw him out the bar while I was hanging with some friends. We exchanged numbers and ended up dating for a while. Unfortunately, his bad boy behaviors, drugs, and alcohol ruined our relationship. He was still the same skinny, pale boy from middle school.

Although I lost my first love my eighth grade year, I still had boys that filled in the gaps at church. This one was very dark-skinned and extremely aggressive. He was adopted. His mother always had hot breath, so every time she spoke to us at church, I would stand back a few feet. I never found him attractive, but I never dismissed his attention on me. At this point, my body was relatively skinny but athletically built. I would go to the bathroom, and when I would come out, he would be hiding in the church coat room across from the ladies' restroom. He'd whisper, "Keshia" to get my attention. I would walk over to the door, and he would tell me to come inside while rapidly beckoning for me to move faster to ensure I was out of view of the sanctuary. The way the church was set up, the glass doors were in the middle of the aisle. If you sat closer to the middle aisle, you would be able to see me. Luckily, Mother sat near the aisle next to the window. When I went into the coat room, he would put his lips all over my mouth and his hands down my skirt. He was a terrible kisser. He never inserted his fingers inside my private parts, he just rubbed aggressively. This would happen almost every Sunday.

We even did this in the car while Mother drove him and his mother home from service one night. I was so bold, but yet so timid. I didn't like him at all, and I heard that I wasn't the only one he was doing this with at the time. I guess I needed to feel like someone wanted me. I still had a crush on the boy with the thick gray glasses, but he had his eye on another gem. She was really pretty with soft, luscious black hair and light skin. She had perfectly straight white teeth, and when she smiled, her dimples were as deep as a cereal bowl. All the boys would goggle over her, and they had every right to do it. Her family was very wealthy. They were very conservative and made sure she and her siblings were noticeably intact every Sunday. There was a point in time when I wanted to be just like her. However, I couldn't compete. Mother was too poor, and you were not around.

The eighth grade dance was my last event I had to attend, before feeling like my life as a teen was three fourths over. I got my hair cut and curled for the dance. I remember the beautician saying, "You got that snapback hair, girl." This meant that my hair was not afraid to go back to its natural state once water or humidity hit it. Nappy. This was our last hoorah before going into high school, so I had to go out with a bang. When the beautician was done with my hair, I looked somewhat like an adult, and everyone loved it. I felt pretty.

Although the dance was one of the best highlights of my eighth grade year, besides basketball and track, things weren't getting any better at home. There were still arguments and distance. Mother and I were at war. My hate for her grew stronger, and as my sister got older, my hatred grew for her, too. I wasn't sure why I hated my sister. We had nothing to talk about, because she was nine years younger. It was bad enough that I didn't get a lot of attention when I was the only child, so adding another person in the equation meant that I was invisible. It wasn't fair, and I kept wondering why I wasn't born to another family.

I remember my father only came around for a few days that year, and Mother acted differently. She was much happier. When he left, it was like he took her happiness with him. I recall getting a phone call a few years later. It was my father. He had moved to Georgia and married someone else. He had her say hello from the background. I didn't know her to hate her, but I was curious to know what about this woman made him want to marry her and not Mother. Once again Mother, my sister, and I were back to being alone. No more phone calls and no more visits for a long time.

Before I went on to high school, things got so bad at home that I wanted a way out. Mother and I had an argument that sent my emotions over the edge. At this point in time, I didn't have a job, and I didn't have a car to go anywhere. I was so angry from my argument with Mother and the absence of my father, that I walked into the kitchen and grabbed our largest and sharpest knife. My eyes were filled with tears as I pressed the knife up against my wrist. I slide the sharp edge across my wrist a few times, but there was no blood. There was just a deep imprint of a line. I put the knife back into the draw and went to my room. I cried myself to sleep, hoping I would never wake up.

Chapter 3 - Cherry

I turned fourteen years old and was on my way to high school – well, the freshman academy. I remember getting my hair cut again. This time it was even shorter. My English teacher who had the same haircut stated that she liked the look on me. It fit my facial structure. My haircut attracted boys, too. Even though I had broken out of my shell toward the end of my eighth grade year, when I got to high school, I pulled myself back in like a turtle pulls its head back into its shell. The freshman academy was much bigger than middle school. Although I was in the freshman center, I got to see the upper class juniors and seniors when they would come over from the high school for vocational courses. I was only able to see them because I was an office aide. Some of them, I recognized from my sixth grade year in middle school or from church. There was one boy who I particularly recognized, because all the girls thought he was good looking. His features hadn't changed since the last time I saw him. I remember it like it was yesterday. He had dark hair and a perfect nose. His hair was close to a buzz cut but not quite. He seemed to have a little swag to him, since he didn't dress like the preppy white boys I was used to seeing. He had a pretty smile, and he was one of the finest white boys I had ever laid eyes on in my life.

Since I was the office aide, there was a list of duties that I had to fulfill, and one of them was passing out school pictures. I had seen his picture in the pile and remembered he was an eighth grader when I was a sixth grader. Although I didn't know much about him in middle school, I knew one thing for sure - he was the definition of sex appeal, and every girl loved him. He dated a popular cheerleader, and she was every boy's wet dream. I delivered his picture and didn't even look at him when I handed it to him. My heart was beating too fast, and I was scared of what would happen if I looked him in the eyes.

Maybe I would pass out or say his name wrong, so I hurriedly walked out the door without uttering a word.

Every time he walked past the office, I would just stare at him. He wore a leather coat and always carried a black binder. He never looked into the office and never said anything to me until one day when we were in the hallway at the same time.

He said, "Wassup."

I replied, "Hi," as we passed each other.

Oddly, he turned around and asked what my name was, and I told him. He told me his name, and I thought to myself, *I already know what your name is, because every girl wants to be with you.* I just smiled at him and tried not to show my nervousness. Then, in the next moment, he did the unthinkable. He asked for my number.

Of course, Mother never had a house phone, and technology wasn't up to par. Therefore, cell phones only worked if you bought minutes, or you had to use a payphone if you had neither a house phone nor a cell phone. I couldn't take the risk of saying I would call him, because there was no guarantee that I could come up with fifty cents every day to do so. I knew we went to my grandmother's house every day, so I gave him that number. He scribbled it on his notebook and said he'd talk to me soon. I walked away thinking, *did the hottest boy in the entire school just ask me for my number? Me? But why?* I wasn't sure what he saw in me. I didn't have the best clothes. My hair was starting to grow out from the cut, so trying to make it look nice and neat was a hassle when getting ready for school at 6am every morning. I knew I wasn't the prettiest girl in school. I mean, who would want the smelly, dark-skinned, short-haired girl?

The school day ended, and I rode the bus home as usual. When we made it to my stop, I got off the bus and started walking home as I normally would do. Every day, a row of cars filled with sophomores, juniors, and seniors would come flying down the street. A white car was among the group, but it was no different from any other car. For some reason, it stood out this day. Once the white car passed, the cutie I had just given my number to at school stuck his head out of the window and flashed his pearly whites. My heart skipped a beat. I couldn't wait for Mother to get off work, because I knew we were going straight to grandma's house. I was going on my first date.

I sat in the small kitchen in my grandmother's two bedroom duplex. Every time the phone rung, I could feel my heart beat very fast. All my cousins and aunts were there, so the noise volume was extremely high. My chance of hearing the phone ring and answering it first was not going to be easy. I went to my grandmother's room where the noise was a lot lower. The phone rang.

Before I could grab it, I heard one of my cousins yell out, "KESHIA! PHONE!"

I picked up the phone and heard a deep tone say, "Hello."   "Hello," I replied.

"You trying to kick it?" he asked.

"Uh yea," I replied nervously.

"Where do you stay at again?"

"Well, I'm not at home. I'm at my grandma's house. She lives on Lakeside."

"Well, me and my boy can pick you up from there then."

"Ok."

I hung up, walked downstairs, and told Mother someone was coming to pick me up. I never told her it was a boy, because I didn't want to hear her mouth.

He pulled up with his boy in the same white car I would see flying down the road every day. I walked out of my grandmother's duplex hoping no one would come out of the house behind me showing their true colors. The windows were tinted, so I couldn't see anyone in the car, but I knew they were staring at me. *Can things get more awkward?* When he opened the door, I hopped in, and all I could see and smell was smoke. Not knowing that I had asthma, he kept smoking his cigarettes, and I just stayed quiet and prayed that I didn't have an asthma attack.

When we drove away from my grandmother's home, I didn't know that this boy would change my world for the worse. Since homecoming had passed, he brought up the subject and asked, "Why didn't you ask me to homecoming? I would have went with you."

I laughed in my head. *Why would I ever ask him to homecoming, when he could go with anyone?*

"Well, I just went with my friends. I had fun," I replied.

"Do you smoke?" he asked as he continued to puff his cigarette.

"No," I said hoping he'd give my lungs a break.

Our conversation was short, because the music was playing so loud in the car. I still remember the song that was playing. It was Outkast, *Sorry Ms. Jackson.* Apparently, he loved music, because he rapped every word. At the time, I didn't know what the hype was about this song, so I just stared into his eyes while he easily impressed me by imitating Eminem. After driving around all day, night fell. I knew Mother didn't have a house phone, so I didn't even attempt to let her know my whereabouts.

We finally pulled in the back of the Blair's Cleaners parking lot and listened to music. He popped another cigarette in his mouth, and I was still taking in it all in that I was actually sitting next to one of the hottest guys in high school. His two boys ended up getting out of the car to smoke cigarettes and use the bathroom. The *Sorry Ms. Jackson* song continued on repeat. I scooted closer to him as if I was going to lean in to kiss him. Instead, I slowly put my hand over his middle area and began to rub on the outside of his jeans. He smirked and continued to smoke his cigarette. Since he didn't stop me, I went forward and unbuttoned his pants and pulled it out. Since I had already been through the whole oral sex phase and vowed to myself I would never do it again, I just stroked it up and down.

Being new to this, I didn't know that I was being aggressive until I asked him, "Does it feel good?"

He replied, "Yea, but it hurts a lil bit."

I immediately stopped and started thinking, *OH NO! I am ruining my chances with him!* I was so embarrassed that I didn't touch him for the rest of the night – well, not in that area. We kissed for a little bit, and then his boys got back in the car. At the time, I wasn't aware that they got out of the car for us to have "alone time." Go figure. I knew it was getting late, and I didn't want Mother and me to fight when I got home, so I politely asked if they would take me home.

After that night, he and I continued to see each other. While Mother was at work, he and the boy who came to pick me up in the white car came over one day after school. I could remember how embarrassed I was from the moment he asked to come over. We didn't have cable, and we didn't have a house phone. Our furniture was really old, and I was hoping Mother had used her food stamps to stock the kitchen, so I could offer them a cup of juice. When they came, I opened the door and immediately ran to my bedroom. He was so attractive that I could barely look him in his eyes, and I damn sure couldn't look at him now, considering how my place reminded me of how poor we were. I let out a deep breath and walked back into the living room. He sat there with his leather coat on, and his boy was sitting next to him with baby blue eyes and gelled down hair. I sat down on the loveseat and pulled my feet under my butt to an almost Indian-style position. We had small conversation, because I wasn't sure what to say. I was fourteen, a freshman, and being cool like the other girls in my grade was a hard task. This was only the second time we hung out, and if my mouth couldn't yell out *awkward*, my body language sure did.

Apparently, he didn't seem to be bothered by the condition of our apartment, because after they left, he was back over a few days later. This time he was by himself. I made sure my twin bed was made up when he came over.

It was a dull colored flowered comforter that had stains of my menstrual cycle, because I wasn't exactly a professional at timing when it would come. I had one single pillow that was stained with hair oils from my nightcap coming off at night because of my wild sleeping arrangements. My sister's bed was next to mine. She was always at daycare whenever I got out of school. It was only a five minute ride from Mother's job, so she could get picked up when Mother got off work.

He came straight back to my room. We talked for a little bit, and then he laid back on my bed. I got on top of him fully clothed and looked into his dark brown eyes. He gave me that same smirk again, and I leaned in to kiss him. I could feel him getting hard, and I knew things would only escalate from there. He sat up suddenly, and then laid me down. He kept on his sweatshirt that was under his black leather coat and unbuckled his pants before he pulled them down just below his butt. I pulled down my pants and spread my legs open. I couldn't believe this was going to happen. I was getting ready to have my virginity taken by the hottest guy in high school. Not to mention, he was an upperclassmen, and you had to be pretty special or popular to pull one of those. I was neither.

I held my breath as I felt the hard tip press up against me. I wasn't sure what it was going to feel like, but I was willing to take the chance. I wanted to feel important. I wanted to feel like someone wanted me. I wanted to feel like my skin didn't have to be lighter and my hair didn't have to be long. I wanted him to tell me I was the only girl he thought was beautiful. As he started to push, it was like he had hit a brick wall. When I looked up he had the facial expression of concentration with his eyes closed, determined to reach his goal of taking my virginity and climaxing. After a few more attempts, I could tell it was not going to go the way either one of us had planned.

During his last attempt, I suddenly heard a car horn. I knew who it was before even attempting to look outside. I said with my eyes as big as a fifty cent piece, "It's my mom!" He immediately jumped off of me and quickly pulled up his pants. I swiftly pulled up my underwear and pants, and we both ran to the front door. He got to my apartment front door first. As I followed him out, I told him to go out the right side of the parking deck to ensure Mother wouldn't see us come out together. I locked the door, and then ran to Mother's station wagon. I remember how proud she was, because we had been without our white Plymouth van for a while due to a blown transmission. I didn't see him walking, as we were driving away from the building. I wondered how he got home. Fortunately, that didn't matter, because I was in clear. Mother had no clue that her little girl was on her way to becoming a woman.

****

When I found out that I was able to get a job with a worker's permit, I jumped head first into finding a job. Mother didn't have the money to get what I wanted, nor could she take care of us. The way I saw to survive was to get it on my own. I locked down a job at my middle school as a janitor. It was a difficult job. Between scrubbing floors, cleaning windows, picking old chewed up gum from under the bottom of the classroom chairs, and emptying trash cans in hot, humid weather, hard work was an understatement.

Since I worked with all males, we laughed and joked all day long. Majority of them were a grade or two older than I was, so I didn't see them as much. Luckily for me, one of them came over to the freshman center, so I was able to get a ride to work. He drove a white Grand Prix, and he was quite a nerd. He wore wired frame glasses, and he was extremely skinny with piercing blue eyes. Since he'd hit puberty, he had acne, but he was very nice to say the least. We would often stop at his house, so he could get a few things before work. I only went inside a few times, and he offered me something to drink. I would always decline. I wouldn't say much, because I would be too busy admiring his home, wishing we could live in a home that was similar to it. At that age, I thought anything other than an apartment was superior, regardless of how it looked.

When we all arrived at work, we would have different hallways to clean. It wasn't my ideal job, but I knew I had to hustle my ass off in order to get new school clothes, keep my hair done, keep the electricity on, and deodorant stocked. High school was just an upgraded version of middle school, and I didn't want to be bullied again if I could help it. Since I knew I wasn't going to try out for the track team until spring of my freshman year, I continued to work. My supervisors were able to let me take a leave of absence when track season started, and then I would come back in the summer. Fortunately, I didn't have to choose between being an athlete and working to keep a roof over my head.

I remember when I ran my first 100 meters. It was during track practice. My hair was still in a short cut. I didn't wear any gloves. I had black and white Nikes on my feet instead of spikes, and I wore an oversized sweatshirt and basketball shorts that showed my ashy chicken legs. It was so cold outside, but Mother couldn't afford any cool jogging pants outfits, so all I had was a drawer full of hand me downs to get me through the fifteen-second race. The coaches and other upperclassmen didn't know me. I stayed quiet but followed whatever commands the track coach yelled out.

There were about three or four coaches, and they all were freshman teachers. I didn't have any of them for classes, so I couldn't pull the teacher's pet move. The head coach who was a science teacher stood at the start line, and the other teachers stood at the finish line with stop watches. I didn't know who was faster than I was, nor did I know if I was faster than anybody in my group. I just knew I could run. When the gun shot off, I darted out of the starting block as fast as I could and ended the race in second place. I didn't know the white girl next to me was that fast. After I got my time from the coaches/teachers at the finish line, I walked away to prepare for the next race I had to run. The coaches asked me my name but nothing further.

It was a couple weeks before our first track meet, and the days were getting warmer. I was able to wear a sports bra, but I still ran in my basketball shorts that covered my knees. Although I was good at running, making the right healthy eating choices were not at the top of my list. One day while doing a hard work out, I had to stop because I felt extremely sick. After my last sprint, I ran off the track into the infield and threw up. The head coach saw me laying there with my eyes closed, gasping for air. I didn't have an inhaler, and my stomach was not letting me get back up to finish my cool down before we had to get back on the bus to go back to the high school. We didn't have a track at the time, so we had to use a local college's track.

As he tapped me on my shoulder to get me out of unresponsive daze from feeling sick, he explained that had I thrown up pure sugar. He was right, because I'd actually had a couple of packs of fruit snacks just before practice. As I tried to catch my breath, I finally got out the words to say, "I can't do this anymore." At this point, getting second place in the 100 meter dash and winning the 400 meters race was not worth it. The cold weather and the hard workouts were wearing on my body. Furthermore, if fruit snacks could make me this sick before a workout, I wanted no parts of running.

The head coach grabbed my arms and pulled me up. Since I could barely stand, leaning over was the best that I could do. He asked if I was ok. When I reassured him that I was, he informed me that I'd made 4x100 relay team. Excitement was going through my mind, but my body had no energy. Although, I had almost just quit the team, I gladly accepted his offer. I walked away slowly when I was finally able to stand up straight. I knew things in my life would change, because not only did I make the team, I was VIP and a Varsity level athlete. I was the definition of a double-edged sword.

For some reason, when you become an athlete, your level of recognition changes and the special treatment from others becomes noticeable. I wasn't used to hanging around kids with money or the ones who lived in lavish homes that made my neighborhood look poverty stricken. I was invited to track parties. Since I was the only freshman on the relay team, anybody that I encountered in my immediate circle was two to three years older than I was. I became cool with a girl from the track team. I'm not sure how our conversation started, but I noticed her because she had big brown eyes and long brown hair. She was a distance runner, so we really didn't have anything to talk about since I was a sprinter.

She had a bubbly personality and a distinct laugh that revealed her two front teeth. Since she was two years older than I was, she was in the same grade as the hot boy who attempted to take my virginity. Since he and I didn't talk since he left my home after hitting a brick wall, I figured she was my way back in with him. The advantage of having her as a teammate and now a friend, was that that she had a car. She was able to take me home after my track meets and track practice. We only could have our funny laughs and conversations during these times, because I didn't have money for a cell phone, and a house phone was out of the question.

Once the conversation came up about the hot boy who attempted to make me into a woman, she confessed that he was the hottest boy in the school and every girl wanted him. I told her that he came over with his friend that drove a white two-door car. She knew him, too. As we talked further, she finally asked if I wanted to go to a party with her. Of course, I wouldn't turn down the offer, despite what Mother had to say. Her parents were very strict and wouldn't allow her out past midnight, but I was ok with that, because I had no reason to be out past that time either.

It was the second week of April, and we were a month in with our track meets. Although I was skinny, my body was in the best possible shape. I had been to a few parties with my new friend. I had even tried alcohol, which didn't turn out well, considering how I was hanging out a car door throwing up off Mike's Hard Lemonade. I also recall going to a house party where the hot boy who almost took my virginity was. I didn't have enough courage to speak up when he was in my presence because I was buzzed off Zima. That night was a blur, but I do remember crawling to the doorstep to get inside the house.

We arrived at our next party at a house that was close to my home. The weather was the perfect temperature. We went inside, and I was as sober as I could be. She introduced me to everyone, and I waved my hand. I spotted the hot boy who attempted to take my virginity sitting at the dining room table, and I still didn't say anything. I just knew I wanted him to notice me, but I didn't know how to make it happen. I had on wide leg jeans with a tube top. I'd curled my nappy hair the best I could. It had been over six weeks since I had a relaxer, so I had to do my best to make it work. They played cards, watched TV and sat around talking about the high school hook ups.

As the time approached midnight, she asked me if I was ready to go, because she had to be home. I didn't know anyone in the house, and I wasn't even sure if I was going to even say anything to him, but I told her to go ahead without me. I was going to walk home. She asked me a second time to make sure I was positive that I could get home. I assured her that I would be okay, and she left to get home before her curfew,

As I sat on the couch for another hour, I started to feel out of place. I got up and started walking toward the door. He got up at the same time and went to the doorway of the upstairs bedroom. As I looked back to see where he had gone, I heard him say my name in a low tone. I followed his voice, and he waved his hand for me to follow him upstairs. I didn't even hesitate. I followed right behind him. It was a dark upstairs bedroom with the exception of the light from the TV. There was a bed to our left and a futon in front of the TV. We sat on the futon. We barely had a conversation, but I remembered laughing at something funny he said. He began to tickle me, which I wasn't aware at the time that it was the "get in your pants" moment. I took the lead and got on top of his lap. We began to kiss. He and I both pulled my tube top over my head, and he started sucking my ping pong sized breasts. Normally, I would have been uncomfortable due to the numerous encounters with the boy who I walked home from school. However, for some reason I thought I was ready to go forward. In my mind, I couldn't stop thinking that this was really happening, and I was okay with it. Well, at least I thought.

Since my jeans were tight, I attempted to unbutton them. I can remember him looking at me.

Then he asked, "Are you ready?"

My response was, "Yes."

He turned off the TV and walked me over to the bed. I pulled down my pants and my floral print underwear. I laid down in the bed, and he pulled his pants down but kept on his shirt. He climbed on top of me, and once again, I felt the hard tip press up against me. Since he knew that he would be up against a brick wall again, his push was much more aggressive. In that split moment, I knew I had made a mistake, but I felt it was too late. I started to feel a burning sensation down there, because I was so dry. Finally, he broke through with one last push, and I could feel myself panic because I was no longer pure.

He sat up and said that he was hurting because of the pushing. I told him I was done and that we could stop. This episode might have last 3-5 minutes. When I got up, I felt pain between my legs like someone had kicked me right in the pussy. He turned on the light, and as I started searching for my clothes, he asked if I was on my period. As I responded with the answer no, I looked at the bed and discovered a puddle of blood. My eyes got extremely big, and my heart started to race. Not only had I lost my virginity in a stranger's house, but there was also proof. After he looked at my face that showed signs of devastation, he shrugged and said, "Don't worry about it. I just popped your cherry."

I didn't even know what that meant, nor could I gather my thoughts. I had just lost my virginity, bled everywhere it seemed, and I was in pain. This was not how I thought it was supposed to go. On top of that, we didn't protect ourselves. We went back downstairs, and I felt like everyone knew what had just taken place. As I started to leave, he asked me to wait because he and his boy who lived in that house would take me home. I agreed and stood at the door. I could see a smear of my blood on the bottom of his shirt. He sat at the dining room table with a smirk on his face like he had just won the lottery. We walked to the car, and I jumped into the backseat. The pain was so bad that I struggled to walk to the car. Getting in to sit down was something that I wasn't prepared for. The car ride was no more than three minutes long. I stayed quiet while he and his boy blasted the music in his light blue four door Honda. I didn't even know what time it was, and I didn't bother to check. All I wanted to do was get home, so I could clean myself up.

We pulled up in the back of the apartment complex, and he turned the music down. He turned around and told me goodbye and said to hit him up. I said bye and ok as I slowly got of the car, hoping he and his boy didn't notice my struggle. As I tried to walk with straight posture and not with my legs so wide apart, I turned back to see if they were watching me walk away. They were. When I got into the house, Mother was snoring, so I crept into the bathroom to put on a pad. My underwear was filled with blood, and my eyes began to water. I waddled to my bed with a little limp and slipped under my floral comforter. I couldn't hold back anymore, and tears began to flow nonstop. I cried myself to sleep and promised myself that I would never do it again.

Chapter 4 – Mission Complete

I probably bled and cried for three days straight after I lost my virginity. I still couldn't believe I had done that. I called and told my aunt who was only related by marriage. She was the cool aunt of the family, because she was always open with her children. The other kids leeched onto her because of her non-judgmental, relaxed personality. I was very envious that she was not my mother and wondered why mother couldn't be like her. She was married and had two teenage daughters that were around my age. She always kept their hair styled, and she dressed in the most current fashion. Deep down inside, I think Mother wanted her lifestyle, because we were at their house every day. My grandmother hated it and blurted out one day, "Your mother is going to ruin her welcome. She needs to stay at home sometimes." The reality is, I think Mother and I both hated being at that apartment. We had next to nothing and barely made it every month off of retail wages and welfare. So, being somewhere else other than home was like a vacation, even if it was only a twenty minute drive.

I always went over to my neighbor's apartment to use the phone, because Mother still didn't have a house phone. Our neighbor was Mother's old high school friend. She had a daughter who was couple of years younger than I was. My mother's high school friend worked full time at a parking garage and drove a gray Aero van. It was quite funny looking. She was never married, and her daughter's father was not a part of their lives either. I was told that her daughter's father was the only man she had been with intimately. She and mother had similar stories, so they could relate in a lot of ways.

I picked up the phone and dialed my aunt to tell her the news. I couldn't really explain in detail, because my neighbor and her daughter were in the living room watching TV, and I couldn't spill my secret to them. After I said so many code words, my aunt didn't hesitate to tell me how disappointed she was because of my actions.

She asked, "How do you feel?"

I responded, "I feel ok."

Then asked, "Was it what you expected?"

With an honest response, I replied, "No. It actually hurt really badly."

My aunt proceeded to tell me that she wished I would have waited, but it was too late. What was done was done. She didn't gripe me out too much. We hung up the phone, and I headed home. Since I couldn't tell Mother what happened, I had a little journal that I jotted a couple of thoughts in every now and then. I ran into my room and started throwing miscellaneous items around on my dresser as I searched for my journal. I don't remember who bought it for me, I just knew I needed it. When I finally found it, I grabbed it and immediately flipped to the back and wrote down the day it happened. I wanted to remember that day for the rest of my life. It was the day I felt like a woman. It was the day I felt loved.

I continued running track for the remaining two months of the school year. Despite the pain of my sexual encounter, we had sex a few more times, and I would write it down afterwards. One night, he walked over to my apartments while Mother was inside. I had to meet him across the street, because I couldn't let Mother know who I was meeting. I made up a lie that someone from the track team needed to see me. I walked across the street to where he was sitting. He didn't have on a shirt. I was excited to see him, but I told him that I couldn't be outside long, because Mother would wonder where I was. We instantly started kissing, and then I put my hands down his pants. We both knew what that meant.

Where we were sitting was in open view, so anyone who walked out of the apartment complex could have seen us from the parking deck. After we kissed for a little longer, he pulled my hand and walked me over to the field behind the plaza. It was a cemetery. I could see the outline of his penis sticking out. I knew what we were going to go do. There were no lights, no people, and no sound. I laid down on the grass next to a headstone. I knew my back was going to have welts on it since I was allergic to grass, but I didn't care much. He pulled down his pants and laid on top of me to position himself to insert. It didn't last very long, and I was ok with that. Being with him and feeling like someone wanted me was all that mattered.

Once he finished, he got up and pulled his pants up. I asked if he had come inside of me.

He replied, "I pulled out onto the grass, so don't worry."

We kissed and he left to walk back home, and I went back inside to Mother. She didn't ask me anything. The coast was clear.

When summer came, I was in heaven. I went back to my job working as a janitor. I would get off a couple hours before Mother did. I could remember one particular day so clearly. It was like a hundred degrees outside. I put on the shortest shorts I could find in my drawer and a striped blue and white shirt. It was my favorite shirt, because it was similar to spandex material and my boobs looked great. My hair had grown out from my Halle Berry haircut, so I was able to curl and swoop my bangs and pull the rest back into a ponytail. He walked through the parking deck and came into the open court of the apartment complex, as I came around the corner to meet him. His hair was freshly cut, and his body was super tan because he wasn't wearing a shirt. He gave me this bad boy gaze, and I fell right into it. I jumped up and greeted him with a kiss to the lips. I walked him inside and was happy to tell him to have a seat on the couch. I had cleaned up the apartment and made it look as nice as possible. Mother had gotten her food stamps, so I was able to give him a can of Pepsi instead of some sugary Kool-Aid I barely knew how to make.

We sat and talked for a short time, and then everything seemed to be routine. I climbed on top of him just like I did when we first had sex and started to kiss his forehead. He pulled my favorite shirt over my head and laid it on the floor. He then reached into his pocket and pulled out a condom. It never occurred to me that this was our first time using one. I let him put it on, and then sat back on his lap. For some reason this felt different to me. My eyes rolled into the back of my head, and I couldn't keep my mouth closed because the feeling was overwhelming. I began to drool down his forehead, and before I realize what happened, he wiped it away probably thinking it was sweat. This was most definitely my first time climaxing. He asked me to get up and get on my knees while still on the couch. I did as I was told and didn't think twice. As he pulled his pants down, I turned around momentarily while he was pushing back and forth. He had a blank look and seemed focused. When he was done, he left my apartment. That was the last time we ever had sex.

One day Mother came home from work, still dressed in her red and khaki. I was in my room wearing nothing but a bra and underwear. She never came all the way into my room. She usually only stopped at the door, but this day was different. She came in and slightly closed the door behind her. What she said next, I didn't expect.

"How long have you been sleeping with him?"

I was so shocked that she even knew there was someone in the picture.

Since I didn't have a response and needed an extra minute to think of one, I put this confused look on my face and said in the faintest voice, "What?"

Mother repeated herself, and I still couldn't think of anything to say, so I immediately began to cry. Through my tears, I mumbled that I was sorry and didn't know why I was having sex.

Mother just looked at me and said, "Stop sleeping with him or else I will call the cops."

I was so embarrassed and didn't know what I was going to do, because I felt that if I lost him, I'd lose everything. No one else paid me any attention in high school, and the little bit of attention I did get was from one of the hottest white boys who graced this Earth.

As I walked into the bathroom to stare at my bloodshot eyes in the mirror, Mother quietly said, "We are going to have to take you to the doctor."

She had a look on her face of fear as if her fourteen year old daughter might possibly be pregnant. It was a bit of sadness and worry that I never seen before. Whenever our electricity got disconnected, I never saw her sweat. We would just pack our bags and head to grandmas until she could get the money to pay the bill. Mother rarely showed emotion, and if she did, it was few far and between. From the look in her eyes, I knew I had hurt her, and I would do anything to take it back. The reality was that I couldn't, and things would just get worse from that point going forward.

When we got to my grandmother's house, I had to break the news to him about Mother finding out and threatening to call the cops if we had sex again. I really didn't think she was serious, but I was just telling him because I needed to vent. Apparently, he saw things differently. I didn't think he would take it so seriously, but he did. After that call, I tried to call him a few more times, but he would never return my calls. When school started again, I was at the high school as a sophomore, and he was a senior. I saw him standing outside of the cafeteria looking as sexy as ever. I walked up and said hello. He didn't seem like he wanted to interact with me at all, because I was getting the cold shoulder and short replies.

In some part of our conversation, I mentioned what Mother said and his response was, "It's cool. I'm about to be eighteen soon anyway."

I didn't want things to end between us, and I had hoped he would not take Mother so seriously. Unfortunately, he did. One day while he was walking through the halls, I had been fed up with his unbothered attitude and how he basically acted like I didn't exist. When we walked past each other in the hallways, I would have rather been stabbed in the stomach than to be ignored by the guy who made me into a woman. I purposely waited by the lockers closer to the auditorium until he came around the corner from his class. I pulled one of my friends to the side to pretend I had something important to say, and right as he passed me, I yelled out his name.

He turned around with arched eyebrows and in the nasty tone, he spat, "SHUT UP, BITCH!"

At first, I just stood there speechless, because I wasn't expecting that reaction. When he walked away, I took a few minutes to gather my thoughts, then stormed after him. He had already reached the main hallway where everyone gathered to get the latest gossip and see their friends that may have been in other classes. I slammed my books down in the middle of the floor and started screaming profanity at him. My girlfriend pulled me back and told me to go to class before the teachers came and took me to the principal's office. Not a lot of people had seen me express a lot of emotions, so this was a total shocker for myself and the rest of my peers. I picked up my few books that I slammed on the floor and headed to math class. My heart was beating so fast, and I fought back tears that were mixed with embarrassment, anger, and pain. I knew it was over between us, and there was nothing I could do about. Not only had I pissed off the boy that I was in love with, but I had also made a complete fool of myself. I thought it made sense at the time, but looking back on it, I looked like the obsessed girl who didn't have enough self-esteem to move on after a break-up.

A few months later, he went to prom with a mixed girl who was selected to be on the homecoming court and asked him to go with her. I still wasn't over it, so I booed in the background when the MC announced them coming into the gym. Every time Mother drove us to grandma's house, I would see her car in his driveway when we would ride past his house. I knew they were having sex, and I would stare out the window feeling sick to my stomach. Mother never knew where he stayed, so I didn't have to worry about her telling me not to look in that direction. Their relationship was short-lived, because he began dating a girl in my grade. We weren't friends, but I knew of her. She had dark skin like mine, and she was very uppity. She gave off the impression that she had money, and she hung out with the "other" crowd who smoked cigarettes, drank alcohol before the legal age, smoked marijuana, and snorted cocaine. She found out that I was upset about their relationship. Although he had already made it clear that we were through, I finally chalked my losses and moved on with my life.

Math wasn't my strongest subject, and when it came to my geometry homework, I made the boy at work finish it for me. In my geometry class, I sat next to a boy with bluish, grayish eyes. I knew him from middle school, so I knew he would be a really good partner in case we had to do group work. His father died in a car crash, and his mother remarried one of our assistant principals at the beginning of our eighth grade year. He once told me in our seventh grade science class that he wanted me to be his girlfriend. I didn't pay him any attention, because he was a little on the chubby side, plus his father did not condone interracial relationships. One of his older stepbrothers and his biological younger brother ran track with me, so I got to see them on a daily basis. The entire family was quite attractive, even down to the dogs. His mother was a petite woman with short hair, and his stepfather looked like he could be an actor in the movie "The Godfather." His brothers looked like models out of a Calvin Klein catalog.

Although I didn't find him attractive in middle school, he had definitely changed physically since then. He had a physically fit body, and he sported a sort of "boy next door" haircut. After we completed our first assignment together, I began to look forward to geometry class on a daily. He was really good friends with my cousin, so I knew that was my way in with him. One day after school, he invited my cousin and me over to his house. His parents weren't home, and Mother just dropped us off and kept rolling. She didn't even question why I would be going over to a house with two boys. She might have thought that because my cousin was there, nothing would happen. She was wrong.

His house had high ceilings with tall windows. It looked like a house off the show "MTV Cribs" compared to Mother's small apartment. We went downstairs and looked around at the sectioned off basement that had a weight room, living room, pool table, bathroom, and his older brother's room. We didn't get to go upstairs, but there was no need. I knew his home was something out of a dream come true. At some point, he and I sat on the couch while my cousin stayed in the weight room. We had begun talking, and it suddenly led into a kiss. I don't remember exactly what we were talking about, but his bluish, grayish eyes had me falling fast. I wanted to show him that I was interested in him, despite what his father taught him about only dating within his race.

I touched his penis, and it was bigger than I had experienced. I knew my cousin was around the corner listening, but I didn't care because he was cute, and I didn't want to miss the opportunity to show him that I liked him. I got down on my knees while he slowly unzipped his pants. I looked up at him and gave him the sexy girl eyes, and then I began to suck away. At some point, I believe my cousin looked around the corner and saw more than he wanted to see, because he waved his hand to tell my cousin to go away. I should have been ashamed of letting my cousin see me perform oral sex, but I didn't care. I just didn't want him to tell Mother, and he didn't.

We stopped after five minutes, and I got up while he zipped up his pants. My cousin came around the corner minutes later, and basically pretended nothing happened. Oh well. We heard the alarm chime and the front door open. "Sexy Eyes" told us that his mother had come home. I had never seen her before, so I didn't know what to expect. As I walked upstairs, he was in the middle of asking his mother if he could have money to order pizza. She began to give him the money, before she turned around as she heard me exiting the basement. When I came through the basement door, her expression was as if she had seen a ghost. I wasn't sure if she was more shocked because her son had a girl over to the house, or because I was black. Needless to say, she ordered our pizza. After we ate, Mother came back and picked my cousin and me up.

Despite meeting his mother and her ghastly expression, I felt I was in love. After that day, he continued to come over to my house. He drove a white Honda. I would always perform oral sex, but we would never have intercourse. He would dry hump until he ejaculated, and I was okay with that, because I really wanted us to work out. He was super cute and seemed to come from a better lifestyle than I did. Based on his frequent appearances, he seemed interested in me. Mother was always at work, so I had plenty of time to spend with him before she got home. He told me that he would always tell his mother that he and I would be studying. It always worked.

The following year, we had chemistry class together. We continued to "study" together. I was so bold, that I started to physically touch his penis underneath the desk when we sat in class. It would get him excited. Homecoming was approaching, and I was hoping he would ask me. Unfortunately, he had his eye on someone else, and she eventually became his girlfriend. She was white with big boobs and long, silky jet black hair. I didn't think she was that pretty, but apparently it didn't matter, because I didn't look any better. He went to homecoming with her, and I took a hard punch to the gut when we couldn't "study" anymore. Fortunately for me, one day he found out that she cheated on him, and he came running back to me to get even with her. I fell into the trap, and before long, we started "studying" again.

One day after school, he took me to his friend's house, and "studying" went further than I expected. I was okay with being the only girl there, because I knew all the boys who were present. I assumed they had never dated outside their race and were surprised to see their boy with someone who didn't exactly look like them. After we sat in the living room together, he and I eventually went into his boy's bedroom. I remember seeing a bunk bed when I went into the room. I was always jealous of people who had those beds, because I always wanted one. We climbed onto the top bunk and started to make out. I pulled down my pants while he pulled his down. He put on a condom, and I laid there feeling like I was the luckiest girl in the world. He inserted and I could feel my body shutter at the intense feeling. His faced turned red, and his mouth opened as he began to thrust in and out. I whispered moans into his ear as he continued to thrust. I happened to look out the window and saw a truck pull up and a woman hop out. She had dark shoulder-length hair, and she was very attractive from what I could see.

While he was lost in the moment, I quickly brought him back to reality and asked, "Who is this woman who just pulled up in the driveway in a truck?"

With a shocked look on his face, he blurted, "Oh! That's his mom!"

We quickly got up and tried to put our pants back on as his boy barged into the room, frantically informing us that his mom was home. I was half-dressed but managed to get it together by the time his mom made it in the house. We greeted her and eventually left. It was a close call, but my mission was accomplished.

I was still working as a janitor at the middle school, when a new guy began to work there. He had blue eyes and perfect white teeth. He wore his hair spiked and had a funny personality. I didn't really talk to him in school, although he was only one grade higher than me. He didn't play any sports, but he knew I was on the track team and congratulated me on being undefeated. We were the team to beat at federal, district, and regional track meets. No one could stop us. We dominated the track, and I especially had every reason to put my all into my sport. The struggles at home were never-ending, and my love life was non-existent.

I believed my boss hated him and didn't think his jokes were funny. I always laughed, because he lit up the boring work environment when he was around. One day while working, we were able to take a break to eat lunch. I didn't pack anything, so I walked past the gym toward the vending machines. I heard voices coming from the gym, so I stopped to see who was in there. All of the boys were sitting on the stage where all the weight lifting equipment was located. They were goofing off as usual. They must have been in there for a while, because everyone was ending their lunch break and heading back to work when I arrived.

As I started to walk away, the new hire asked me where I was going.

I turned around and shyly said, "Back to work."

"No. Stay here with me for a while," he replied.

I figured that staying in the gym an extra few minutes wouldn't hurt. The lights were off, so the chances of someone finding us in there was slim to none. I walked up to him while he sat on the weight bench. We talked for a little bit.

Then, he said in a quiet voice, "Come closer. Why are you over there?"

I didn't hesitate to follow his orders. I thought he was fairly attractive and didn't think there were be any harm in sitting on his lap. As soon as I got within arm's reach, he took his hand and started feeling on my backside, before putting his hands inside my tear-away pants. At the time, thongs were starting to become popular, but I didn't wear them unless I was on the track, so full sized underwear were a must in my wardrobe. I could feel him getting hard while I was sitting on him. I touched it, and then put my hands inside his pants.

As he leaned his head back and opened his mouth indicating that he was enjoying the warm touch of my hands, I slid down onto my knees. I pulled it out and began to suck savagely. I told myself I would never do it again, but I hadn't had any interaction with a boy in almost a year, and the craving to satisfy the need of intimacy was bubbling over the top. The cold hotdog I used for masturbation while Mother was at work only gave temporary satisfaction. It was nothing like the real a body pressed up against me. I didn't understand why I thought it was okay to use a hotdog for climaxing, but my body was reacting in a way I wasn't used to, and the feeling I got was just too much for my adolescent body to handle. I needed that satisfaction. I wanted to be loved. I wanted someone to want me. This was my moment.

After he was done, I could feel the wetness on my hand. I never saw it, since it was pitch black in the gym. I wiped my hands on the inside of my shirt and went back to work. Although we saw each other in school, we never said a word or spoke of our shenanigans. We eventually did have sex in the same spot that I performed oral sex. We even attempted to have sex in one of the classrooms on the second floor of the school building. I didn't know anything about anal, but he must have been quite familiar. He attempted but failed. I wasn't comfortable letting him do it, but I never stopped him because I was too scared.

One day before track practice, I heard him talking to one of my teammates. She was a hurdler like I was. She had long blonde hair and pretty blue eyes. What was most unique about her, was the scar she had that started from her forehead and went around her cheek. Surprisingly, it never took away from her beauty. I loved her parents. They were always at the track meets. Her mother was a massage therapist and would rub the track runners' legs if they felt tight before a race. He tried his hardest to take her out, but she wasn't budging. I think she thought he was really weird and wasn't at all attractive. I liked the weird ones. I thought to myself, *how could he be asking her out, when he was just trying to have sex with me at work the day before? Why didn't he beg me to be with him? She wasn't interested anyway. At least I showed that I was interested by having sex with him.* Needless to say, I realized that I was not on the top of the list of girls he wanted to take to prom, so I did what I did best. Moved on to the next guy.

Chapter 5 – The Star

Track and Field during my sophomore year was great. We made it to state and placed third. When it came to athletics, no one could tell me a thing, because I was a beast when I touched the track. Unfortunately, my parents were never there to witness my greatness. I sucked it up though and continued to show up and show out. We dominated in the 4x100, 4x200, and 4x400 relays, winning federal league, district, and regional championships. I was also a hurdler. Even though I was the federal and district champion, regionals were tough, because the girls from the inner city schools out of Cleveland where a force to be reckoned with on the track. They held the state title, and surprisingly, they were really nice to my team and me. I think it was because two of the girls on my relay were white, and they were the only two white girls on the track running sprints. They had to give credit where credit was due. My white girls were fast. Unfortunately, after those fast white girls graduated, our team became mediocre. The relays were not the same without them.

During my junior year, we didn't place as high at state as we did the year before. I still did well individually. I became athlete of the week and couldn't be more stoked. While I was the track athlete of the week, so was the boy who took my virginity and called me a bitch. He got athlete of the week in baseball, and they put us in the newspaper at the same time. I was literally sick to my stomach. My coach tried to force us to go to their state game to support the success throughout their season, but I made it clear that if I had to go, I would sit on the bus. Needless to say, he dropped it, and we never went. Good.

I was doing a little bit better academically. Since I was an athlete, I got out of taking a chemistry exam and pretty much was never penalized for late or incomplete assignments. All juniors and seniors had to be in vocational classes, so I chose the administrative office technology program. It had a lot to do with using a 10-key calculator, fast typing, and an extensive workbook that dealt with banking and other sections that involved counting numbers. I chose the program, because I knew I would never be an auto mechanic nor a cosmologist. I figured that having office skills would be more useful than those other two options if I wanted a decent job after high school. Luckily for me, I didn't have to be a janitor for long, because we were able to get paid jobs while we attended school. Because I had built a relationship with the teachers and principals at the school despite them knowing that I had sex in their gym the previous year, I was rehired as their office aid. The only problem was that I didn't have enough money saved to get a car, and I had no clue how I was going to get it. If I couldn't get the money who was going to take me to work when Mother was already at work? I was on a mad hunt to find a car that was less than a thousand dollars. I only had three hundred dollars saved.

One day I noticed a blue two door car as mother and I drove past an auto-mechanic shop. I figured it couldn't hurt to look at it, so I made Mother stop one day while we were on the way to grandmother's house. The price was twelve hundred, and I tried to quickly calculate how many paychecks I had to save in order to purchase the car. I ended up calling the owner and asking how much he wanted for his car. His original response was twelve hundred dollars, but after talking further, he explained there was a part that needed to be fixed on the car. I had never negotiated anything in my life, and I really was not sure how to get the right words out. Although I was only a junior in high school, I managed to talk him down to nine hundred dollars. When I heard the word *DEAL*, I knew I had to step my hustle game up to get the remaining six hundred.

I knew I was getting paid three hundred dollars that week, but I still needed three hundred more. I knew Mother didn't have it, but I remember her calling someone, possibly my grandmother, to let her know that I made a deal to get my first car. I called everyone I knew, but no one had an extra three hundred dollars to loan me until my next paycheck. Needless to say, I waited it out and finally got the six hundred dollars saved to purchase the car. I was super broke, but I knew I needed this car to take a load off Mothers' back and to get to work.

While I was on a high from purchasing my first car, I never got the part that it needed. After a few months, it began to stall and the steering wheel would lock up before the car would suddenly shut off. One day while I was leaving my grandmother's house, my car began to stutter, and I knew that meant bad news. I sped as fast as I could to get home, because I knew the car would do its shut off routine. When that would happen, I couldn't start the car again until the next day. It was so cold and snowy outside, but I couldn't slow down. I just knew I needed to get home before I became stranded.

As I flew down the back road past my high school, I went over a little hill that accelerated my car, causing me to slam into a semi- pickup truck that was parked next to the apartment complexes. There were two random girls standing outside and saw me crash. I remained seated for a few minutes, trying to analyze what had just happened. I could see that my hood was pushed up closer to the windshield. As I attempted to get out of the car, the door wouldn't open. That's when it hit me that I had crashed, and I began to cry. I didn't have a cell phone, so I asked the girls who had watched me fly down that road, if I could use their phone. I called Mother and told her my location and what happened. She called our neighbor, and they drove together to save me from my crisis.

Mother looked devastated when she arrived on the scene. All the hard work I'd put into saving money to get this car had withered away. I called my job the next day and told them I was not able to come to work due to the wreck. I was so hurt about losing my car. To help out, the principal came and picked me up every day for work until the students went on Christmas break. She was a short lady with dirty blonde hair, and she wore oversized business suits and had a fast-paced walk. I was embarrassed about my accident, so I didn't tell many people. One of the people I did tell, sat next to me in English class. She was very tall with long dark brown hair that was almost to her butt. She had perfect white teeth and an upbeat personality. I never saw her without a smile. I am not sure how we became friends, but apparently her glowing personality managed to get me to spill the beans about my car. Not to mention, she was one of the people on my list to call when I was asking for three hundred dollars to purchase the car. I must have been desperate.

When I told her with tears in my eyes that I crashed my car, she quickly responded by offering to come to my house to comfort me. I was so upset that I agreed to her coming to Mother's small apartment. I was so embarrassed when she arrived. She claimed she didn't care and brought Wendy's chicken nuggets to cheer me up. I wouldn't even let my best friend come into my house. I guess my wrecked emotions from the car accident and her bringing over Wendy's made all my insecurities about my living conditions disappear. Our friendship grew from there.

Luckily for us, my car problem was solved a few months later when Mother got a substantial amount of money back from her income tax return for being a single parent. I could always tell when she got it, too. We would go out to eat with my grandmother more frequently, bills were always paid, and if we were lucky, we got cable and a house phone for a few months before we started to get shut off notices. I had already had my license. I had been practicing my driving skills in Mother's white Plymouth van. Once I got good at driving, Mother would ask me to drive her home each night after we left my grandmother's house. I quickly grew tired of driving Mother home, because it didn't matter if I was tired, I still had to drive. I didn't complain to Mother, because I knew that the excited feeling would come back once I got my car. It wasn't too long after I perfected my driving skills, that Mother went to a "buy here, pay here" lot and purchase a 1996 cherry red two-door Saturn for me. It was a moment I thought I'd never experience.

I actually felt important and a part of the cools kids in school. I went straight to my best friend's house to show her my new car. She had a two-door burgundy Buick Regal with leather burgundy seats and a cd player that was hooked up to the radio by a cassette tape. She was so excited when she came outside and saw it. She asked to drive, and of course, we were off cruising the streets. I didn't have a cd player, but that was okay. A car was a car, CD player or not. I was just glad I could get back and forth to work without worry. Unfortunately, I had to factor in paying car insurance and my own gas, but somehow I managed with $5.25 an hour.

Since I was now mobile, I was able to have a little freedom when it came to the boys. I wasn't dating anyone in particular, but my insecurities of wanting to be loved always won. I normally preyed on the boys who were quiet and really never had any experience. However, those who preyed on me normally weren't my type. When I first saw him, he was kind of on the short side. He had pretty blue eyes, but because he'd hit puberty, acne was his best friend. He would always talk to me as we passed each other in the hallways at school, and he seemed very nice. He drove a massive 4x4 truck that I knew wasn't his, but it was pretty nonetheless.

My apartment building was next to a car wash that I would frequently visit. Mother still didn't have a house phone. If my neighbor wasn't home, I would collect fifty cents to use the pay phone located in their parking lot to make an important phone call if it couldn't wait. I can't remember how we got in contact with each other to meet up, but we got the job done.

He pulled up in the parking lot, and I jumped in his truck. It was dark outside, and I made sure Mother wouldn't look out her bedroom window and see us in this truck. We talked for a little while and eventually started kissing. I knew he had never been with anyone sexually, and I was determined to be his first.

While we were kissing, I unzipped his pants and put my hands down his pants. His penis felt weird. Different. As I stroked up and down, there seemed to be an excessive amount of skin. I thought I was pulling on a rubber band because his skin stretched so far. When I put my mouth on the tip and slid down slowly, I felt all the loose skin in my mouth. I had never felt anything like it. I took off my pants and sat on his lap while he sat in the driver's seat. He laid his seat back, and I positioned it to insert. I went up and down a few times, before he suddenly stopped me.

"Keshia, I just don't...I'm not ready."

With a confused look, I replied, "Okay."

"I want to be in a relationship first or wait for marriage."

With the same look, I replied, "Okay."

The moment turned really awkward, and before I knew it, I was pulling up my pants and running into the house feeling dumb as hell. He didn't want me either. Years later, I saw him at a gas station after we had both graduated from high school. I might have been twenty-two or twenty-three at the time. He was still driving that 4x4 truck with lawn equipment strapped to the back. He immediately recognized me and hopped out of his truck.

"Hey Keshia, how have you been?"

"Oh, I've been great, getting ready to graduate from college. How have you been?"

With a smile, he replied, "Oh, you know, nothing new. Just got my own lawn care service thing going on, but that's it." I finished pumping gas and closed my gas door.

"Hey, it was nice to see you, Keshia."

"It was nice seeing you, too."

I got in the car and drove down Market Street wondering, *what was I thinking?*

After our failed sexual encounter, I knew I wouldn't have another chance to be alone with him to talk about how things went, but it didn't matter. I had my eye on someone else. He was also short. He had dark hair and was very quiet around me. When he was around his friends, he was a little obnoxious, but it didn't bother me. He was very attractive to me, but my best friend disagreed. He was friends with her brother. Every chance I got to be around my best friend, I hoped her brother was near just so I could get a chance to see him. He and I never really talked in high school either. He would say one or two sentences to me here and there. I think he found me attractive - at least that was my interpretation. Since I was mobile, I drove to his house one day. I am still not sure how we were able to see each other, since cell phones were few far and between. I don't even know how I got to his house without a GPS. My sense of direction must have been superb back then, because traveling somewhere today requires advanced technology.

I had just came from a track meet, so I quickly drove home to change clothes and get ready for a hot and heavy night. People were already there when I arrived. He must have had a house party, and his parents apparently didn't care. I know if it was Mother, she would have slapped me into the middle of next week. I didn't know that group of kids, so my words were limited. A few of them recognized me from track, but my focus wasn't on them. It was very dark inside the house. It seemed that everyone had already had a good time, and they were now in the relaxation phase from either smoking a lot of weed or drinking a lot of alcohol. I had never smoked, and my first experience with alcohol during my freshman year ruined the chances of me waking up with a bad hang over.

Since everyone was mellowed out, he asked if I wanted to go outside, and I quickly agreed. We hopped into my small two-door Saturn and talked for a few minutes. The next thing I knew, I was taking my pants off and straddling him in the passenger seat. He put on a condom, and once again, I found myself going up and down, breathing extremely hard while letting out loud moans. His face looked blank, and he didn't utter a word. When we were done, he pulled up his pants, and I felt relieved as I sat staring at him. We both said goodbye, and that was our first and last verbal and sexual encounter. Years later after high school, I saw him out at a nightclub with his old high school friend.

"Hey Keshia, do you remember him from high school?"

I was shocked to see him, but I acknowledged his presence with a head nod. His response was a simple *hey*, and we left it at that. I later found out he made a racial slur about a white girl dating a black guy. I thought to myself, *oh, he must have forgotten that he slept with me in high school.* So, anytime I see him, I walk past him as if he never existed.

My relationship with Mother had not gotten any better. It was my sixteenth birthday, and I got neither a gift nor a party. Hell, I didn't even get a *happy birthday*. I sat at home and did nothing. I was so heartbroken, because turning sixteen was a big deal, and Mother didn't even recognize it. Actually, I don't remember her recognizing any of my birthdays besides my eight and tenth birthdays. I had a birthday party at McDonald's for my eighth birthday and got my first bike. When I turned ten, I invited my friends and family over for a swimming party. I knew she didn't have the means to get an extravagant gift, but I at least wanted her to acknowledge that it was my birthday. She didn't. Christmas was the same way. I knew the only way we got gifts was through charity. The program was called Adopt-A-Family. I never met the family that bought my Christmas presents, but I am forever thankful. The electricity bill was caught up, and we had food. Since I was working, I could contribute when Mother was struggling. I didn't have to worry so much about food, because Mother got plenty of food stamps. When the new school year rolled around, I had to buy my own school clothes, too. Since I wore micro-braids all the time, spending money on my hair became a bi-yearly responsibility.

Besides the daily responsibility of providing for myself, it was prom season, and I didn't know if anyone was interested in taking me. Although I had a great body with a firm booty, ripped six-pack, and muscular structure, I didn't feel as pretty as all the other girls. I really wanted to go, since I had only been asked to go to a dance one time my entire high school career. I normally went with my girlfriends, but prom was different. To me, prom was like the dress rehearsal for your wedding day. Although marriage was not on my mind at the time, I wanted to feel like a man came and swooped me off my feet as he carried me off into my happily ever after.

Needless to say, I found a date. Mother was so mad, because she did not want to me go with the guy from our church. He played the organ and always wore suits and dress shoes to school. He was very dark-skinned and had a little gap between his two front teeth. Some people thought he was homosexual, but I refused to believe it. Honestly, I felt he had a crush on me, but I never asked. I didn't care. I just needed a date, so I could feel important like the rest of the girls. Mother and I went to a fancy boutique shop that was located ten minutes away from our apartment. The dresses were really expensive, but this was my moment to shine. I had always wanted to wear a ball gown, but since my waist was so small and my body was in shape, I wanted to show off my nice body. That's the only attractive quality that I felt I had. The dress that I really liked was light pink and it had three pieces. It was a halter top that stopped right above my belly button, and the skirt flowed to the floor with a split up the left leg to my mid-thigh. The beaded shawl that was long to the floor was pretty much pointless, but I rocked it anyway.

I didn't know if we had a dress code for prom, since showing our mid-drift was a no-go during regular school hours. I used the shawl as protection. My hair was a totally different battle. Since I didn't wear makeup, the only money I knew I had to spend was on my dress and hair. It was still track season, so taking my hair out of the micro braids was not an option. Luckily for me, my aunt was able to pin my braids up into a French roll with a few curly braids hanging down by my ear. Needless to say, I was able to cut out that expense.

Since I was still on the track team, the boy from church and I went with another track couple. They picked us up from my Mother's house. We took pictures outside in the gravel parking lot, and then drove off to meet the other upperclassmen at an extravagant restaurant located near a lake. I really didn't like the food, and it was definitely out the price range for my date and me. Thank God they had chicken tenders, because I might have only ordered a water if I didn't see anything I could pronounce. When we arrived at the dance, I almost immediately started socializing and dancing with other people.

My date and I weren't very close friends in school, so I didn't feel the need to stay with him all night just because he was my prom date. He wasn't my dream guy anyway, so there was no need to entertain him at all. We did manage to slow dance to one song, so my job was done. After the dance, my track teammate and her boyfriend took us home. The church boy wasn't my ideal prom date, or should I say not the ideal person I wanted to have sex with, but I'm glad I was able to dress up for a night and feel good for once before the school year ended.

Chapter 6 - Transition

I celebrated my seventeenth birthday during the summer of my final year in high school. The older track girls from our state qualifying team had graduated, and I was promoted to captain of the girls' team. It wasn't the best year for us, because the freshman and sophomores were not as fast, and our chances of going to state were slim to none. Luckily, we still had one fast junior who broke records all over the county and even qualified for state in the 100m race. She was a beast, and I envied her talent. She was so gifted, and I was just good. Although being a good athlete is acceptable, being gifted was another level. I wished she would have taken her gift as seriously as I did, but unfortunately she didn't. Boys, boys, and more boys were her only focus, instead of a full ride scholarship to a division one college. If I was that gifted, that would have been my focus. However, my focus was survival and finding someone to love me.

The brown-skinned boy who wore the thick gray glasses and always went to church with his grandmother, was finally a senior in high school. I was still shy when it came to speaking to him. He was a great basketball player at this private high school, and all the girls loved him and his team. He started to develop a relationship with my aunt. Since I was praise dancing with my aunt's daughters at the time, it wasn't difficult for us to run into each other. My aunt would attend his basketball games, and of course, I would tag along. She loved supporting kids who were doing good things and staying off the streets. Mother, on the other hand, hated him with a passion. Neither she nor my grandmother could understand why I was so infatuated with him. Honestly, I didn't know either. I just knew he was attractive, and I was in love and no one could tell me differently.

My aunt had already told him that I had feelings for him. I'm pretty sure he was already aware, since I was always at his games and full of energy. I wasn't sure if he was seeing other girls, but our guaranteed day to see each other was Sunday. I could sense that he had feelings for me, and I was willing to be as vulnerable as possible to let him know he could take me whenever he wanted. I finally lucked up and got a chance to hang out with him. Since I wasn't eighteen yet, we went to a club that allowed teens to party like adults minus the alcohol.

I would hear all about the kids going, so I was excited about this being my first time. I lied to Mother and told her that I was staying at my aunt's house for a sleepover with her daughters. He and his homeboy came to pick us up, and off to the club we went. There were hundreds of kids waiting outside to get in when we arrived. This was my first club experience, and I was very overwhelmed. There were so many cute boys all around. I felt like I was in boy heaven, until my insecurities quickly stepped in and ruined my excitement. I felt I wasn't dressed in the latest fashion, and my hair wasn't long enough. I knew that I couldn't compete with the other girls.

It looked like wild animals were running loose when we entered the building. There were various nationalities, ages, and sizes of people. Boys and girls were showcasing their dancing skills on the stage. It was definitely my type of environment. Although I was very quiet, I took pride in my sexualized dancing skills. BET was one of the few channels that showed a semi-clear picture through Mother's fuzzy TV screen. I would study videos after school when I didn't have track practice, so if someone wanted to dance battle that night, I was game.

Our group split up, when we finally got inside the club. I saw kids from my high school as I ventured off and danced with boys that I didn't even know. At one point, I circled the crowd a few times to track down someone in my group, when I came across my "date" dancing with someone else. I was heartbroken. We weren't officially together, but since we came together, it felt like we were on a date. I kept my cool, but I was burning with envy inside. When he was finished dancing, I made myself visible as he high-fived all his buddies. I think he knew I was uncomfortable, but we never spoke of it afterwards. He took us back to my aunt's house, and although I was bummed about him dancing with another girl, I was satisfied with spending time with him.

Christmas was quickly approaching. Even though I knew I wasn't getting any presents from my family, I knew I wanted to get him something. We had sex a few times after our appearance at the club, and I was more in love than ever. I didn't think it was a one-time deal, since he and my aunt were close. I assumed his respect level for me was quite high. I had never spent money on a boy, but I wanted to express my love anyway I could, since Mother would not allow us to date. I was sneaking out of the house to see him every chance I got. I would be gone for a few hours even on a school night. Mother was a heavy sleeper, so leaving at any time was not hard to do.

The same thing would happen at night when we would talk to each other on the phone. By this time, I had convinced my next door neighbor to put me on her cell phone plan with Verizon. I paid $45 a month. Mother didn't have good reception in our apartment, so I would stand up on my bed up and lean against the window to make sure I got reception to prevent missing his call. Since it was a few days before Christmas, I needed to do last minute shopping for Mother, my baby sister, and him.

I didn't have anything in particular that I wanted to get for him, so my final decision was to purchase a Cavalier's hat. He loved wearing snapbacks, therefore I thought this would be a great asset to his wardrobe. I had to give it to him at church, but I had to make sure Mother wasn't around. She probably would have lit the hat on fire, if she knew I spent my hard earned money on a boy that she didn't like. When I gave him his present, he was very appreciative of my kind gesture, and I knew for sure this would make things become official between us. Unfortunately, that was not the case.

After giving him his present, not too long afterwards, I discovered he had a girlfriend. She was brown-skinned and had the longest chin ever. The joke was that she had a Jay Leno chin. She wore brown contacts and had big boobs - the area in which I was lacking. She worked at Taco Bell and eventually started showing up at his basketball games. I was so disgusted that I ran into the bathroom at church when I found out about his girlfriend.   I called my aunt sobbing like I was the wife who just found out her husband cheated on her. My aunt was quite surprised by this disclosure, because he told her everything. When I say everything, I mean everything. I eventually found out that he decided to be with her because he knew Mother didn't like him. He knew I was never able to go out, because Mother kept me sheltered from the real world, so she thought. I wasn't taking no for an answer. I knew I was in love with him, and this was the only boy I had ever wanted to be with, so I chose to stick around regardless of his new girlfriend.

The next school dance was coming up. It was called Turnabout. This was the dance where the girls asked the boys to attend the dance. Since he attended another school, I had to get a permission slip approved by my principal. I was nervous to ask him to come to the dance, but I sucked up my insecurities and called him anyway.

"Hey, I have to ask you something."

"What is it?" he asked puzzled.

"I don't know how to say it," I replied nervously.

By this time, I could tell he was growing impatient.

In a slow, quiet voice, I asked, "Will you go to Turnabout with me?"

After a few seconds, he replied, "Yes, I will go with you to Turnabout."

Although he had a girlfriend, I was so relieved to still be able to go to a dance with the person I've always loved. I didn't tell Mother, and I was hoping she would never find out, since he was driving us to the dance. I just lied and said other friends were picking me up. We got to the dance, and I saw our names written in gold on paper that was shaped like glass slippers. I was proud of that piece of paper. It was the first and, unfortunately, last time our names would be put next to each other referencing us as a couple.

Since his team made it to the playoffs for basketball, I was still attending his games with my aunt and her daughters. I went to the bathroom during one of the games and began talking to a blonde haired girl who knew me from running track the year before. She worked at Taco Bell with his girlfriend, and to my surprise, her cousin was the boy who had the extra skin on his penis. We talked for a few minutes when I came out of the bathroom, and before I knew it, his girlfriend walked up. We didn't say anything to each other. She just glared at me like I stole something from her. Word on the street was that she knew I took her boyfriend, the love of my life, to a school dance. Although I played the lackadaisical role, I was hurt deep down inside, because I wanted to be his girlfriend. However, because Mother hated him and was very strict on my whereabouts, she had the upper hand. The title didn't stop me though. He and I continued to see each other. He came to Mother's house on a few occasions, and I went to his grandmother's home where we had sex. He joined the track team, so I was able to see him for those events as well. Unfortunately, she was not lagging too far behind.

When we had to run at track meets with all the county schools, she would come with a group of friends and glare at me from across the stands. I got fed up with her looks and contacted him so he could check her about her eyeballs. He put us on a three-way call. She didn't know I was on the phone until he informed her of such. She insisted that neither she nor her friends look at me. After that, we didn't have another issue.

I was nearing the end of my track career. I qualified at state in the 4x100, but that was it. I wasn't really seeing anyone besides the boy from church, even though he had a girlfriend. He was leaving for college soon, and I didn't know when or if he would return. It didn't matter, since I had my own plans ahead of me. I began to grow close with one of the track families. They were a huge family that consisted of three Caucasian children, two Vietnamese children, one Asian child, and one Korean child. Diversity clearly was not an issue. The stepmother had short sandy-blonde hair and intense blue eyes. Her new husband had polished white hair. They were very friendly and always offered me something to eat when I went to their house. I refused because I wasn't used to eating anyone else's food besides my family's food. To keep from being rude, I always opted to eat cereal. I had been going to their house for the past four years that I was in high school. The mother was my ninth grade teacher, and her children all went to high school with me. One of her sons was in my grade, her daughter was on my relay team, and I didn't know her youngest son very well, because he wasn't in high school yet.

The husband was a dentist, and the Vietnamese, Asian and Korean children were his adopted kids from his first marriage. Two of the four children ran track with me. The middle daughter was very quiet, therefore I didn't see or hear from her often. His son who was mentality handicapped was the star of the school. Not knowing him, meant you didn't know their family. Although, they had seven kids already, they took me on as their eighth child. I was fine with that, because they lived in a mansion in my eyes. Their grass was so plush, that it felt like a bed when we'd lie down on it. They had a three car garage while I was only used to carports or unpaved parking lots. Their entire basement was bigger than our apartment. Each of their kids were well-behaved and seemed to have a good head on their shoulders. It seemed as though life was great for them. Meanwhile, in the back of mind, I was thinking of how Mother couldn't even keep her lights on from month to month.

When I initially began to get closer to the family, the mother's first statement to me was, "Keshia, we need to start thinking about your future. What college are you interested in attending?"

I felt like a deer in headlights, since I really didn't have an answer to that question. All I knew was that I wanted to help people just as the track families helped me. I also wasn't ready to move away, because all my family and friends were still here. I had spoken with the Kent State Track coach, and he was interested in having me run for the team. I was not interested in running at all. All I wanted was an education. I knew you and mother did not go to school past high school, so I wanted to give this thing called college a try.

I took the ACT test and only scored a 17. I didn't know if that was a good score or not. I felt like it wasn't, but I sent it to Kent State anyway. Luckily for me, Kent State had eight small branches, and one was located right in my home town. I filled out my FAFSA and sent all the required information to the school. I have no clue how I figured out how to do it, but I made sure I was ahead of the game. The track mother volunteered to take me to the campus to explore my options. When the advisor asked if I had completed the FASFA, I was proud to say that I did. Unfortunately, they didn't offer a social work major, so I had to settle for a field that was related.

My high school graduation day came, and I remember not feeling my prettiest. Nonetheless, I put on my biggest smile and walked across the stage. I missed graduation rehearsal the day before, because I was at the state track meet. Luckily, my last name was very common, so I knew who I was to stand beside when it was my time to walk across the stage. I spent the summer after graduation preparing for my freshman year in college. I had slowed down on my sex machine behavior for a short period of time, until I turned eighteen years old. My best friend since the sixth grade was headed to play basketball at a four college that was an hour away. We wanted to live it up before she left, so we went to the club. Since we were mobile, we went to any club that let us in that night. We didn't go further than Akron, Ohio, because our jobs didn't pay enough for us to afford to waste gas. Somehow, we still managed to go out whenever we could. It was very fun to experience independence and the feeling of being "officially grown."

School started and I was able to stay focused enough to pull out a 3.0 GPA the first semester. I was going to class in the morning and working part time job at night. At the time, being a telemarketer wasn't a bad job, but unfortunately I wasn't a good sales woman. I had to convince people to donate blood. You would think it wouldn't be that hard, but it was. I had never sold anything but my body, so this was far from a walk in the park. One donator that I called must have realized that I was black once I said my name, because he ended up calling me a nigger before hanging up on me. I wanted to cry, but I held it in. I had only been a top seller one time, but I couldn't get my groove back after that, so they eventually had to let me go because I wasn't meeting the quota.

I was devastated, because I had never been fired from a job before. I didn't know what I was going to do, or how I was going to tell Mother. I had car insurance, and my phone bill was due. I knew Mother couldn't help me out. Fortunately for me, I used my school grant money and purchased a computer. I stored it at my track family's house. To hold me over until I could find another job, they offered to buy the computer from me. I agreed, and they would give me $100 whenever I needed, until it equaled out the cost of the computer. I hustled to find a job until I couldn't hustle anymore. I finally got burned out from searching, and just like that, I picked up a Sunday paper and saw that a new restaurant was opening and hiring for a "hostess with the mostest." I knew they definitely meant me.

I remember wearing the dumbest outfit to my interview. I had on white pants, a flowy light pink shirt with a weird design on it, and these brown high-heeled sandal-like shoes. Although I felt super corny in the interview, my corniness paid off and landed me a second interview. I nailed the second interview.

"We would like to welcome you to the team as one of our hostesses," the general manager stated with such emphasis.

I was elated, and I couldn't wait to tell Mother and the track family who was paying my way through life, that they didn't have to bear that responsibility any longer.

We were required to wear all black, because we were considered the front of the house. During training, we had to taste all of the food on the menu as well as practice seating people at their tables. It felt like this was my first "big girl" job, and I wasn't the slightest bit ready. When it was my turn to seat a table and say our little one-minute speech, I froze up when I walked my co-workers to their table. I got teary-eyed very fast and started to cry. I got so embarrassed that I ran to the bathroom. When I came out, some of my new co-workers told me that it would get better over time. I managed to pull myself together and get prepared for the second segment, which was food tasting.

Part two didn't go well for me, because I was so against eating food that I couldn't pronounce. They wanted us to sample the food so we'd be able to tell our customers how good the food tasted. When the unpronounceable food came to me, I would just pass it on to the next person. I especially wasn't going to taste a piece of bread that had tomatoes and food shavings that looked like paint chippings sprinkled on it. They called it Bruschetta. However, I did manage to eat this breaded thing that looked like it had tentacles. When I bit into it, it was rather chewy but tasted like an upscale piece of chicken with gourmet seasoning. They called it Calamari, also known as fried squid. I was quite shocked that I was eating it, but it wasn't that bad.

I worked at the restaurant with people who had big personalities, and I got my first experience of what it was like to have an older man interested in me. I was used to dealing with high school boys, so this was very different. He was a chubby fella who had these two front teeth that never seemed to stay in his mouth. He worked the pizza section. He would look at me in a way that I had never experienced, and for whatever reason it attracted me. Fast. I was stilling living at home with Mother, so we were never able to go to my house to have sex.

I'd always ask why we couldn't go to his house, and he always said, "My roommate messed up the house, so I can't take you there."

I never questioned who his roommate was or if the roommate was boy or girl. I just settled for having sex in the car. The first time I experienced oral sex was with him, and it was terrible. It hurt very badly, and I had vowed to myself that I would never let a man do that again. The first time we had sex was at a run-down motel, and he was very blunt about this not being anything serious. I didn't care at the time. I just liked the attention he was giving me. We had sex a few more times before I found out that he had a ten year old daughter. He often mentioned I looked like the mother of his child. I assumed she was my complexion, and that was why he was so drawn to me. Later in the spring, I found out that he had a girlfriend the entire time we were having sex. She worked at the bar down the street from the restaurant. Because I was under twenty-one years of age, I was never able to see her. All our co-workers knew he had a girlfriend and never once told me to steer clear. I felt played, however that didn't stop me.

The day had finally come and I was given the opportunity to move out of Mother's house. I had finished my first year of school and was ready to see what the world had to offer. My relationship with my mother had gotten somewhat better, but I was still ready to live freely. I went to her one night while she was sitting on the couch and told her that I was going be roommates with a girl I knew from another high school. She also ran track in high school, and she attended the same campus as I did. On top of that, she was just as dark-skinned and really attractive. Mother agreed to let me move out.

Even though I was excited about moving out, I made sure to ask, "Can I come back home if things don't work out?"

Without hesitation she stated, "Yeah, you can come back home."

Just like that, I was moving out on my own. When I agreed to move out, I didn't know who all I would be staying with, but I quickly found out there were boys involved. They weren't my type, but I didn't mind. I just wanted freedom. At the time, I was only working at the restaurant. I soon figured out that my paycheck wasn't going to cover my portion of the bills, but I managed until I could pick up a second gig.

My female roommate was very much a firecracker and practiced rebellious behavior. She came from a wealthy family and lived in an upscale neighborhood. Her father was a psychiatrist. It was the first time I witnessed a black family not live in poverty. She drove a Lexus SUV to school and indulged in callous activities, such as drinking and smoking. I didn't get into either one of those. She was very impulsive. If she wanted a tattoo or a piercing, she did it without thinking twice. If she said she were going to fight someone, that's just what she did without hesitation. However, I wasn't that risky when it came to pain. Unfortunately, she didn't care how I felt. When she said we were doing something, that's what we were doing.

Fortunately, she also managed to convince me to evaluate my wardrobe. I mostly wore flip flops, gym shoes, or sweat pants. I didn't dress up unless it was absolutely a requirement. I was able to get boy's attention being very basic, so I didn't need to change.

One day she came into my room and asked, "Why don't you have heels? And, why are all your clothes gray, black and brown?"

I honestly didn't have an answer. Most days, it represented how I felt about myself. Very dark.

During my silence, she stated, "Don't worry. We gone change that." Then, she walked out my room raising her eyebrows and wearing a devilish grin. From that moment on, my life took a turn I never imagined.

Chapter 7 – Ms. Independent

Living with one girl and three boys was like living like a reality TV show. We had house party after house party, and drama after drama. Whether it was one of us girls having sex with one of the roommates or their friends, someone inviting a guest to the condo that we didn't like, or someone not paying their portion of the rent on time, something was always out of order. I was still working at the restaurant on the weekends, and I was still seeing the chubby guy who had the girlfriend. I invited him over one night after he got off work, and he surprised me with underwear from Victoria Secret. This was the first time I received an actual gift from a man. We had sex, and then he went back home to his "roommate."

I found a full time job that started at $10.00 an hour working at a factory. My checks were bigger than I was used to, and I felt rich. The only thing that sucked about it was waking up early in the morning and trying to get there on time. I had to be clocked in at 8:00 a.m. They did not play with being late, and it didn't help that we had house parties three to four nights a week. I was juggling being a full time student as well. My hustle was too real. Luckily, my supervisor was really cool. He really didn't care about anything, just as long as I showed up and did my job. I always went to work, but it was never on time.

My job was very tiring. I had to put auto parts in caged bins. The parts were very greasy and sometimes heavy. We were given a list to complete each day. I had to wear a t-shirt with the company's logo on it and my name tag. I always wore my raggedy gray sweat pants with it. The funniest part about me working in a factory was the idea of me using the forklift. I was very good at it, but I had my moments when I knocked bins down a few times. A few other college students worked with me. One of them happened to be the church boy that I was so in love with in high school. He was home for the summer and needed a job, so someone got him hired. I wasn't in love with him anymore. We said hello to one another, and I continued on with my work day like our hot flame never existed. While I wasn't paying attention to him, one of the other boys had their eyes on me. He was brown-skinned with a dashing smile and muscular arms. He drove a nice car with rims and he seemed to be very nice. I was at the vending machine on break one day, and he stopped to make small talk. Although I thought he was attractive, the next question hit me by surprise.

"What's your number?"

As I gave it to him, I was wondering what he could possibly want with me. I figured he wanted someone a lot prettier than me. He looked like a guy that would date someone with long silky hair and light skin. When he finally did contact me, he mentioned that he was looking at my pussy while I sat on the floor during my break. He said he could see the outline of it and it turned him on. I was confused about how he could have seen the outline. The gray dirty shorts I wore that day didn't fit very well. I actually had to roll them a few times, so they wouldn't be so baggy.

A couple of days later, he asked me to meet him at the park that was 15-20 minutes away from my condo. I thought we would be just there to hang out, but I was clearly wrong. When he arrived at the park, his cousin was in the front seat. I recognized the guy, because he and I went to the same high school. I spoke to the cousin before we walked off into the dark shadows of the park. He wasted no time making a move on me. He immediately kissed me on the mouth and abruptly asked me to lay on the ground. Since I hadn't grown out of my grass allergy, I expected to have welts on my back when we were finished. As I laid down, I felt a huge bulge penetrate me. It almost like a cucumber was being shoved inside of my tiny hole. I was so shocked by the size of his penis, that I could hardly breathe while he thrusted in and out my hole. After a few minutes of that, he told me to stand up and bend over. I obliged. It hurt like hell, but I managed to hold out until he was done. When it was over, I got into my car as he got into his, and I went back to the condo. My back was itchy all night.

One night we had some friends over at the condo and things got a little out of control. Two girls got highly intoxicated and wanted to pick a fight. I didn't know them, but my roommates did. I wasn't sure what started the fight, but everyone was trying to get them to calm down. Before we knew it, someone called the cops, and we had to shut the party down. Once the chaos settled down, I spotted a guy with short black hair. He looked like an Italian or Greek version of the boy who took my virginity. He was wearing an oversized t-shirt with dirty white shoes. I was immediately attracted to him but not because of his outdated fashion.

He didn't say much, but I liked them quiet anyway. We had small talk about the fight after the girls got kicked out. As the night went on, he asked if he could sleep over since he had been drinking. Of course I wasn't going tell him no. He slept on the couch the first night. I think he was nervous to ask to sleep in my bed, but that quickly changed. After that, he slept in my bed every night for the following two weeks. He would get off work and catch a ride with his friends. They would come over to drink and smoke. Surprisingly, we didn't have sex during those weeks. He just laid in my bed with me until we fell asleep.

One day after a night of laughs, alcohol, and weed, he turned to me and said, "Keshia, I have been coming over here every day. I think that I want you to be my girlfriend."

I was elated because I really liked him and how he paid a lot of attention to me while we hung out. It was even better that his friends knew my roommates. It was like we were one big happy family. Everything was all good until my female roommate and I decided we would get our own place. The condo was in one of the roommate's mom's name. Since the lease was up, we all had to move. Plus, one of our roommates had mental health issues. He would have angry outbursts and punch walls. He spoke in a monotone voice, and he wasn't much of a ladies' man. He had a nice body, but he had acne issues and only talked about video games and being in the armed forces.

After my roommate and I moved out, my boyfriend still came over to see me after work. Everything was okay at first, and we spent Valentine's Day together. He bought flowers for me, and we went to dinner. We had great sex in the house and outside in the car. By this time, I had gotten rid of my red Saturn. It died on me, and I was in a state of panic. I didn't know how I was going to get back and forth to school and work. Mother didn't have any money. Although I made a substantial amount of money working at the factory, I spent it on bills, food, gas, and revamping my wardrobe. Luckily, the multi-cultural track family still considered me as their eighth child. They knew Mother was not able to get me another car and my father was absent, so they bought me a blue two-door Escort. I called her Blue Betty.

Things were getting distant between my boyfriend and me. He wouldn't come over every day anymore. We weren't the party house like before, nor did we have alcohol or weed to pass around. I had called him to come over for about a week, and he either wouldn't answer or he'd tell me that he was at work. I got so desperate that I went up to his job unannounced. Fortunately for him, he was at work which helped me believe that he hadn't been lying to me.

I asked him where he had been, and he said, "I've been working. I can't talk because I have to go back to the kitchen. I'll call you when I get off."

He never called. The next night, I got fed up and sent him a text telling him that I didn't think we could be together since he hadn't been over to see me. Unfortunately, he agreed and said he didn't want the relationship anymore. I started to cry until his next statement caught me off guard.

"I think you are a better match for my best friend. You two have similar personalities, and I think you guys would be good together."

I was so devastated that he would even think that it was okay to pass me off to his friends. Furthermore, his best friend wasn't even attractive. He wore big pop bottle glasses, had big eyes and teeth, and always wore a Brown's sweater with a turtleneck underneath. He just wasn't for me. I laid on my couch for a week. Of course my roommate wasn't having it and told me to pull it together.

Her exact words were, "There are plenty more men out there. If he don't want you, someone else will."

Her confidence was through the roof. I didn't understand how she was able to be so brave with men while being so dark-skinned. I had the "hustle for a job and education" mastered, but I needed her attitude. From that moment on, I studied what she did, how she carried herself, and what she did to make boys chase after her. I was tired of being used or only having boyfriends for two months. I wanted something different, so I had to change my attitude and my look.

Chapter 8 – The Comeback

My personal makeover began with my hair. Unfortunately, this was a disastrous beginning, because I managed to rip my hair out when I removed my micro braids. My hair was shoulder length at time, but my head felt naked after my beautician cut my ends. The boys didn't like chicks that had short hair, so I needed something different. My roommate wasn't scared to change her look. When she came home and saw my hair struggle, she told me to go purchase a wig. I was so turned off by that idea, but I had no other choice due to the bald spots all over my head.

I went to the hair store where I always purchased my micro braid hair. I looked around timidly until I found a wig that was straight and little past my neck in length. It looked natural enough to pass as my own hair, and the $25 price tag was right up my alley. I put it on as soon as I got home. One of my longtime male best friends came over, so we could go out to the club. He was roughly 6'4" tall and very dark-skinned. We always argued about who was darker between the two of us, but I always knew I was a shade lighter.

He walked up the steps while I was looking at myself in the mirror and exclaimed, "OH MY GOD, LOOK AT YOUR HAIR!! Wait, is that all your hair?"

Shyly I replied, "No, it's a wig."

As he chuckled, he replied, "Yea, I was getting to say that your hair cannot be that shiny and full."

I laughed but was secretly hoping no one else would notice.

I started to get used to the wig after wearing it for a few weeks, and I even bought a couple more to add some variety. They were very convenient and attracted the attention of men. I got double takes and flirtatious greetings. I felt good about myself and the attention I got from convincing people that my wigs were my natural hair. I branched out and purchased curly wigs, which increased the admiration from men. For some reason, curly hair just does something to them.

Since my best friend moved back home because she quit the basketball team, her and I went to our favorite bar and danced the night away. I spotted a sexy guy from across the room. He was handsome with tattoos and cocoa brown skin. To top it off, he had Southern accent because he moved to Ohio from Atlanta. He spotted me looking at him and eventually came over to me.

"Hey shawty. What yo name?"

"Keshia."

"Who are you here with?"

"I am here with my best friend. Who are you here with?"

"I'm here with my brother," he replied.

As he pointed across the room, I recognized his brother from my history class and attending my house parties at the condo. He motioned for his brother to come over. With a big smile, the brother shouted over the blaring music.

"Hey Kesh! Did you study for the test we got coming up next week?"

I just smiled and shook my head. After the last call for alcohol was announced over the mic, we decided to leave. The announcement didn't apply to me, because I wasn't twenty-one yet. My girlfriend was off giving her number to some NBA athlete. At the time I didn't know he played for the NBA, but I later found out.

"Atlanta" came over to me while I was headed to the car and asked what I was doing later. I told him I had to go home because I had to work the next morning. He gave me his number and his brother invited us to come over and play cards sometime. I smiled and agreed that we would. He called me a week later and asked if I could bring a few friends over to take them up on their invitation to play cards. I made my best friend go with me the first time.

When we walked through the door, he was shirtless and I saw his tattooed chest and his six pack of abs. He gave me a flirtatious look that I couldn't ignore. Every now and then, he would look at me from across the table, and I would shyly look away. I can't lie, I was aroused by him being so into me and so attractive. He informed me that he liked "chocolate girls." Luckily, my skin matched exactly what he liked. It was a good night. Although I didn't drink or smoke, everyone around me did. I was having a good time hanging with good people - so I thought.

He called me to come over again, but this time it was just the two of us. I still had on my clothes from the factory, since I'd switched to night shift when school started back up. I didn't care that I was dirty and sweaty, because I wanted to hang out. I drove Betty to the duplex where he was staying with a relative until he was able to get a job and a place of his own. After having a short conversation, things quickly escalated to sex. I didn't want to have sex but I remember laying on the couch, still wearing my factory shirt. He got on top of me, ripped my pants off and then started pushing harder and harder with all his force. He held my hands behind my head. In those few moments, the pain was unbearable.

With a soft voice I asked, "Can you please stop?"

Without hesitation, he answered, "No," and continued to go harder and harder.

I knew if I screamed stop, it wouldn't work out in my favor. I laid there in pain as my eyes started to fill with tears. As soon as he finished, I got up confused about what had just happened. I grabbed my sweatpants and silently walked to the door. I said goodbye and left. I knew something wasn't right, but I didn't say a word. His brother sat next to me the next day at school and asked how my night went. He must have called him, because his brother had a huge grin on his face while I was still afraid to admit the truth.

"So you and my brother did it last night huh?"

I stuttered for a second, "Well, well, we did but it...it was too much. I couldn't...I don't know."

"Ahhhhhhh mannnn, you probably just couldn't handle it that's all. It's cool, Kesh, just admit it," as he chuckled.

In the back of my mind, I was too scared to admit that I felt violated. I just kept telling myself that because I never stopped him, I brought this on myself.

I eventually chuckled and said, "Yea I just couldn't handle it."

To convince myself that I wasn't sexually assaulted, I went back to his duplex the very next week. This time I wasn't going to do anything with him. We sat on the couch for a while, and then he went into the kitchen. He never turned on the light but asked me to come in and join him.

I walked into the kitchen as he calmly stated, "Put your hands on the chair."

At first I was a little confused by the request, so I asked him to repeat himself. I could barely see him in the dark, and I had no clue what he was about to do.

"Put your hands on the chair."

I slowly walked over to the chair and placed one hand on the back of the chair. I was trembling with fear as tears began to fill my eyes.

"Put both hand on the chair."

Although I could not see him, I could hear him talking through his clenched teeth as he grew frustrated with my inability to follow his demands. At that point, I wasn't comfortable with his demands or where the situation was going, so I told him that I was not putting my hands on the back of the chair.

He replied in an aggressive tone, "I SAID PUT YOUR HANDS ON THE BACK OF THE CHAIR!"

Immediately, I knew I had to get out of there. I refused again and began to cry while I walked toward the front door and opened it.

Sounding confused, he asked, "Why are you crying?"

He never got an answer to that question, because I was too busy trying to wipe my tears.

He continued with the next question, "Did you think I was going to rape you or something?"

I shook my head in denial, as if I fully believed he would not hurt me. However, in the back of my mind, I knew I would have been dead meat. As soon as I got back into Betty, I vowed that I would never put myself in that situation ever again. His brother ended up dropping out of school, but we were able to still keep in contact through phone calls.

He called me a few months later and said, "Keshia, I just want to apologize for not believing you."

Confused, I responded, "Believing me about what?"

"My brother raped my sister, and he has been raping her for the past three years. He fled the city, so we are riding around looking for him. When we do, we gone put him six feet under."

With a relieved sigh, but disgusted image, I replied, "Well, I tried to tell you that he was aggressive and something wasn't right."

The conversation ended, and I never heard from either of them again. I never went to counseling after the sexual assault, nor did I disclose it to Mother or my friends. I just continued on through college without a care in the world. I was still going out to the bars every day of the week. Although I didn't drink as much, I was hanging out with people who did. I wasn't into drugs, but my friends definitely were.

By this time, I had gotten into my first physical altercation with a random girl at the bar. I don't know if my anger stemmed from boys using me as their sex slave or the strictness of Mother not letting me be a teenager and making me become an adult faster than I wanted to, but I beat the girl to a pulp. I continuously punched her in the center of her forehead until it split open. Her blood was running down my arm. When her friend broke us apart, I turned around to see a bunch of men standing in the window of the bar next door cheering us on.

Someone in the bar called the police, and I just knew I was going to jail. The ambulance arrived as well, since she needed stitches. I hid my bloody hand behind my back, because I didn't want the cops to know that I beat the brakes off of her. I felt that I needed to demand my respect. I was tired of being disrespected by Mother and boys, and I was tired of being seen as the "pussy" of the group. The cops made my friends and me stand up against the wall until we were granted the permission to leave. Apparently the witnesses outside vouched for us and reported that the other group of girls started the fight, which was true.

We went home when the officer let us go. I remember my best friend calling everyone she could to tell to them that I had gotten into my first fight and actually won. I called Mother and told her I got into a fight, and I started to cry.

Her first words were, "Well, did you win?"

I told her I did, but for whatever reason, I was embarrassed. It was different when my roommate got into fights. I would just tag along but would never have to physically fight anyone, because my roommate could handle her own. This time it was all me. I held my own. I stood my ground and demanded to be respected.

I got into a few more fights after that, but that soon came to an end since I had to move to the main campus to finish my degree. I was so nervous because I had never moved away from home, but I had no other choice if I wanted to be the first college graduate in the family. It was a good thing I was still close to the track family who implanted the initial idea for me to attend school. The dentist also graduated from the college I was attending, so he was very familiar with the area. He drove me up to the campus, and we rode around until we found a suitable place for me to live. The place I found was right across the street from the campus, therefore I could walk to class instead of spending $100 on a parking permit. I had the option to rent a studio apartment that only had a small living space, a closet, and a bathroom. It wasn't my ideal living space, but I had to make it work. Plus, it was $318 a month which was the cheapest place near or around campus. Their one bedroom was $450 a month, and I knew I couldn't afford that only working four days a week for $8.00 an hour at the nursing home. I filled out the application, and the dentist was my co-signer. The leasing manager called me the same day to congratulate me on being approved for the apartment.

Once my lease was up with my roommate, she moved back home with her parents, and I moved in with my aunt for six months. I put my furniture in storage and only brought my clothes, mattress, and TV to put in my aunt's basement. I didn't go back to Mother's house because I knew she didn't have the room for me. Besides, I didn't want to start helping her with the bills, because I needed every coin I earned to be put toward my new apartment. My aunt had three kids, and they were quite crazy. She was a single mother, yet she was more financially well off than Mother thanks to the child support she received for her two youngest children. Her youngest child was my favorite. Since he was the youngest in the family, he was babied by everyone, even me. I would have to drive him to the bus stop each morning, but that soon got old. I realized that I didn't have children and getting up to get him to school was not my priority. That bit of short-lived responsibility helped me realize that I could never be a Mother. I loved sleep too much, and taking care of kids would cut into my sleep.

I continued to hang out with friends as much as possible. I knew our days together were numbered, and the thought of not being with them every day was driving me insane. They were my family, and I counted on them more than I counted on Mother. They were my rock, and I wasn't sure how being away from them was going to help me reach my goal of finishing school. I knew I couldn't be in a serious relationship because I was moving, but one night I stumbled across my middle school boyfriend while I was hanging with my best friend at the bar. He had not changed one bit from his looks to his bad boy behaviors. We spoke to each other and exchanged numbers. One night he called me, and I remember staying on the phone with him for about three hours. He told me that he had never been on the phone with a girl that long nor did he like talking on the phone. I guess there was something about me that made me an exception to the rule.

After a week of phone conversations, he asked me to come over to his parents' home. I remember arriving there and speaking to his Mother. She was a petite Caucasian woman with blonde hair. She had remarried and was no longer with his biological father. His stepfather was sitting on the couch when I arrived. Seeing his parents made me really nervous. I greeted them before my ex escorted me to his bedroom.

As we headed down the hall, I asked him, "Did your parents know I was black?"

He replied, "Well, I told my mom I liked this girl.....and that she was black. She didn't have a problem with it as long as I was happy."

I was able to breathe a little bit slower, but I initially didn't know what to expect. When we dated in middle school, I never met his parents. I just knew his father thought he was a piece of shit that would never amount to anything. He proved his father wrong by going to Culinary Arts School and obtaining his Associates Degree. He was working as a head cook at a new wing restaurant that was less than six months old. I was proud of him. It was the week before Valentine's Day, and we had only been hanging out for two weeks. We had only had sex once, and it went rather well. I went to his house one night after work, and he asked to be my boyfriend. I was caught off guard and knew in the back of my mind that I moving to the main campus in less than six months.

For once, I used discernment and actually declined his request.

He looked sad when I turned him down. I knew I cared about him, and I found him attractive, although my friends did not. He was still tall and skinny with gaps between his teeth. He hadn't grown out of his bad boy act, but it seemed he was in a better position in life, since he had just started a new job and had a degree. He didn't live on his own, but I couldn't judge since I was staying in my aunt's basement. He had a car, but it wasn't reliable. Needless to say, although I turned his offer down to be his girlfriend, we still hung out as friends until Valentine's Day. By then, I'd had a change of heart. I really enjoyed hanging out with him at his mom's house, and the sex was up to standard. Being with him this time was the first time that I experienced someone perform oral sex in my buttock area.

When I had arrived at his home, I gave him a Valentine's Day card and a small gift. He was shocked that I him brought something, but I wanted to surprise him by asking to be his girlfriend, since I turned him down the first time. Luckily he accepted, and it was official. I was in an actual relationship. It had been three years since my last official relationship, and I was excited to see where our relationship was going to go. Unfortunately, my fairytale was short-lived. After I told him I loved him for the first time, the dynamics of the relationship shifted fast. The calls were less frequent, and so were my visits to his mother's apartment. I found myself abandoned and used once again. I was trying to figure out what went wrong with our relationship and how things changed so rapidly. When we finally had "the talk," he was starting to stutter but finally spoke the truth.

"Keshia, I got scared after you told me you loved me. That's not where I am right now. I am no good for you, and you don't need to love a guy like me. That's why I ran when you told me you loved me."

I faced yet another heartbreak, so I went to the bar with my girlfriends that night. I didn't really talk much, but I could remember trying so hard to hold back my tears. I couldn't believe that my middle school sweetheart didn't want me.

I got over it, and he was quickly replaced with a college football player. I met him through a rap group I used to dance for. I was into local rappers for whatever reason. He was very dark-skinned, like Gorilla dark. I found him attractive though. We met at a swimming party at a mansion located forty minutes outside of my hometown. I knew he was interested in one of my other girlfriends, but when I called him out on it, he denied it. I wasn't looking for anything serious since I was still picking up the pieces from my last heartbreak. We exchanged numbers, and within a week I was upstairs in his bed having sex. This went on for a few months.

Sometimes I would receive a text from him asking me to come over. Since he lived so close to my aunt's house, I would literally be at his place within thirty seconds. I would walk in, lift up my dress or skirt, depending on what type of mood I was in and sit right on it. Once he climaxed, I would pull my dress or skirt down and walk back out the door like nothing happened. If I saw him out at the bar, we wouldn't acknowledge each other. It wasn't until one day when I was out at the bar with all my girlfriends for my birthday, and I saw him talking to my friend that he denied he was trying to get with. He kept asking her for her number and trying to convince her to go home with him. I sat as calmly as I could to try and ignore his thirst for my friend. I was just in his bed a couple of nights before, so how dare he make a pass at her knowing I was sitting right there. Being calm wasn't working, so I made a smart comment to him.

Before I knew it, he yelled out in front of the entire bar, "FUCK YOU! YOU WERE JUST A FUCK ANYWAY!"

I stood on top of my chair pointing down in his face and screaming at him, before I was pulled down from the bar stool and dragged away. The people around me told me he wasn't worth it. As I turned around to face the gorilla to see if he was still sitting in his chair, my best friend had gotten into his face. Before we knew it, the gorilla threw a drink on her, drenching her dress in alcohol. Once that happened, he was escorted out by the security and police. My best friend came over and asked what all had happened between the gorilla and me, as she pat herself dry. When we went to the bathroom to regroup, we came back out, the gorilla and his friend were somehow back inside standing by the counter to order food. As we walked by, the gorilla tried to grab my best friend by the arm to plead his case, but she yanked away from him demanding him to never touch her.

When they made last call at the bar, we gathered our belongings and said our goodbyes and thanks to everyone that came out for my birthday. As we exited the bar, I saw two male figures standing up against the back of a Monte Carlo. As I got closer, I noticed it was the gorilla and his best friend. I ignored their presence. I was over it by now, but they were not. While I engaged in conversation with my friends, the gorilla butted into the conversation. I immediately turned around and told him to mind his business and leave since he had gotten kicked out the bar over an hour earlier. While I was yelling and screaming in his face, my best friend who was still wet from the gorilla throwing alcohol on her, took her shoe and threw it at his head. That caused all hell to break loose.

Everyone was holding me back, but as I kept ducking, dodging, and trying to untangle myself from the grips of hands holding my arms. I saw the gorilla throw the black shoe back at my best friend. It landed at her feet, and she charged him. She abruptly stopped in her tracks when he clenched his fist and swung right past her face, just inches from the tip of her nose. I was so furious that with all my adrenaline rushing. I finally broke free from all the tight grips and ran full speed with my fist balled up and punched him upside the head as hard as I could. The minute I tried to go back again for a second round of kicking his ass, an old friend of mine who was 6'4 built like a football player, ran up and cornered him up against the car. He told the gorilla that he needed to leave or else he was going to have to go through him. The 6'4", 250 pound man being in his face got him scared enough to get into the car and leave.

When I finally calmed down, the pain set in. I looked down at my pinky, and the acrylic nail had broken in half with blood rushing to the surface. My pinky was so swollen that I thought I had broken it again. This was the same finger I fractured while playing basketball my freshman year in the gym. At that time, someone had passed me the ball while I was wearing acrylic nails and fractured my pinky. That is the only bone that I have ever broken in my body, and due to the throbbing pain, I felt I did the same thing to it again. I got nervous because I didn't have insurance, and I refused to go to the hospital to get it examined. The only luck I had was to go into the nursing home where I worked and have the nurses on duty take a look at it.

I didn't even change my clothes the next day when I went into the nursing home, nor was my supervisor shocked to see me. She knew I lived at the bar, and this was not the first time she had heard of me getting into a fight while partying the night away. She just shook her head when she saw me and asked what happened. I told her about the fight and that I needed a nurse to see if my finger was fractured. The kitchen supervisors who were present, told me I had to put alcohol on the broken nail before an infection occurred. After a few minutes of convincing, I finally squeezed my eyes tightly while they rubbed the alcohol wipe across my broken nail and poured peroxide in the crack of the nail. The burning sensation convinced me that I never wanted to fight while wearing nails again, nor did I ever want to see the gorilla again.

Chapter 9 – The Graduate

I got all moved into my studio apartment with the help of my father and his new wife. He married a Caucasian woman who had two kids of her own. She had a boy and girl who were twins. She was really nice and seemed to be a good fit for my dad. She told me that my father ranted and raved about how he was so proud of me for doing all the things I was doing with my life. I found that statement to be so ironic, since he never helped me get anywhere in life except under another man as I looked for love in all the wrong places. I had only visited her a few times while she and my father were living together. She seemed to be very supportive knowing that he had seven children and was previously addicted to drugs, in and out of jail, and physically abusive toward his first wife. I am not sure if she knew why he and his first wife divorced, but I was not going to be the one to tell her.

She and my dad went to Mother's apartment and packed all my things in the back of her van. My father had the biggest smile on his face, because he was so excited to help his baby girl move into her first apartment living on her own. I was just excited that he and his wife could help me move. Mother didn't have the gas money nor reliable transportation to help, and I wasn't going to ask the dentist. He and his family had already done enough for me by co-signing for the apartment, buying me a new car, and giving me any money I needed to purchase school books. I needed my father to step up to the plate, and if it wasn't for his wife volunteering, I don't know if I would have moved. Once I got all moved in, that was the last time I asked my father to do anything, because I knew he would disappear. I was on my own and I was ready to get my degree.

School was going well, and I was pulling my grades up because I was less than a year from graduating. I couldn't have been more excited to be the first one to graduate from college on both sides of the family. I was working four days a week and driving back and forth from school to Mother's home. I was interning at a mental health facility the first semester. That was an interesting population, since the majority of my experience had been working with the elderly. Since one of their staff members was killed in a tragic car accident, the two other interns and I were hired and split her caseload. I was excited to gain experience and have extra income. My only focus was graduating, and I was making it happen. I was not as homesick anymore, since I could go home whenever I was ready, and it was only a forty-five minute drive. On top of that, we had our first black president in office, so I felt I could do anything.

There were a few cute boys in my apartment building, and I was able attend a few parties once I befriended them. I was never attracted to any of them, because they weren't my type. One of the guys was a part of a fraternity. He was on the heavier side, but his personality was very outgoing. We met when I was unloading my groceries from my trunk. He tried to make a pass at me, but I was quick to show him my disinterest. Unfortunately, I got a flat tire one night and needed help, so I was forced to go down to his apartment to ask for his assistance. I could tell he wasn't interested in helping me, seeing that he watched me change my own tire. What a douche. A few weeks later, I learned that he had a girlfriend. She was my complexion. I saw the two of them walking out of our building holding hands and thought to myself, *boy, isn't she lucky. Not.*

The other guy I met was African. He wore black rimmed glasses and was on the short side. He dressed very nice, but I had no interest in him either. He too had an outgoing personality. I met him when I went to the student center to get a drink since I had spent the last few hours in the library studying for an exam. He followed me downstairs and proceeded to ask what my name was and where was I from. To this day, because I have dark skin, a lot of men believe I am from the Islands or Jamaica. I always bring them back to reality and tell them I am from a small town just forty-five minutes away. They are usually shocked by my confession about my roots, but I am used to that response. I exchanged numbers with the African guy, and he would call me every so often. One night while sitting in the computer room in my apartment building, he confessed to having a girlfriend, but unfortunately for him, they had not been physically intimate with each other.

With his sexual frustrations about to spill over, he blurted out, "Can I hit it?"

I was so turned off and quickly shut his request down. He immediately apologized and laughed as though that question was a joke. I knew he was being serious, whether he would admit or not. After I turned him down, he never contacted me again.

The other guy I met didn't live on campus. I had actually met him previously at a bar in my hometown. He went to the main campus as well but commuted back and forth. We had sex one time, and he had one of the biggest penises I had ever touched. It was too painful to let him finish, so I made him stop. He was not at all upset by the request for him to stop. He was not aggressive and was very much sympathetic. This guy was very skinny and had big ears. He had a big smile that reminded me of Steve Harvey's smile. He knew I had moved to the main campus, so he decided to call me and ask if he could come over. I made sure I had on boy shorts when he showed up. He drove a two door Chevy truck on rims. It was a little raggedy, but he had a vehicle, so that's all that mattered.

When he got there, he had an upcoming final and needed to study. My plans were different, because I wanted to have sex and not punk out again. Unfortunately, that was not where his mind was. His exam was in an hour, and although he thought I looked delicious in my boy shorts, he stayed strong. He had his priorities straight, while I clearly didn't. I was a little salty that we didn't have sex, but we followed up a few days later and completed the mission. I struggled toward the end due to the pain, but I got through it. I felt accomplished because he seemed to be satisfied. We weren't serious and I was okay with that. He wanted to come over another night to have round three, but his Chevy truck finally broke down, and he wasn't able to come. I told him it was okay, and that was the last time I saw him until one day on campus.

I didn't say anything to him, because we hadn't spoken in a while. We were Facebook friends, so I was able to see what was going on in his life and from the looks of it, he'd turned over a new leaf. I started to see videos of him preaching sermons and quoting bible verses. I was a little taken aback by his abrupt change, but I knew there were no hard feelings between us. I was actually happy for him, although I knew our opportunity to rekindle the flame was long gone. I did send him a personal message to tell him that I saw him on campus but did not speak because I was too afraid.

Reluctantly, he replied with a warm message, "Oh, Keshia why didn't you speak? I would never ignore you, and there is no need for you to be afraid. Whenever you see me on campus next time, make sure you speak. We are friends."

A few months later, he uploaded a picture of him with a girl. She didn't seem like his type. She was oddly shaped and showed more of her gums than her teeth when she smiled. She wore these nerdy glasses and a white dress. I figured she was the "church girl." Needless to say, he married her and the only thing I could think of was, *how is she taking all that dick?*

The next boy I met was another dark-skinned boy who wore dreads. We had met each other in the club a few times, and our interaction never went further than a few dances. Finally one night when I went to hang out with my girlfriends at one of our hometown bars, he happened to be there hanging out with his boys. He was dressed up and caught me looking at him.

I figured he didn't recognize who I was from our previous encounters, because he motioned me over to him and said, "What's your name dark-skinned?"

After I told him my name, I said hi followed by saying his name.

With an awkward look, he asked, "How do you know my name?"

I refreshed his memory by letting him know we'd met years ago at a bar. He didn't recall our meeting but asked to get my number anyway. After that, we met each other on campus, and I went to his house to hang out. We were alone and he offered to show a movie. I actually thought it was going to be a good night until he made a move. I wanted to have sex with him, but I was not prepared and was caught off guard by his aggressiveness. I asked him about the last time he had sex.

His response was, "It's been a month."

I thought to myself that I wasn't going to be the next victim. I just wasn't ready nor was I turned on at that time. I told him I didn't want to have sex and left his house. A few days later, he invited me to a house party he was having. He made it clear that other girls were going to be there, and it would be a fun night. When I walked in, I was greeted by a guy who was feeding women strawberries with chocolate syrup. I wasn't playing that game, so I passed on the sexual feeding. There were at least twenty people present. He introduced me to everyone as his friend, and I shyly said hello. I didn't know anyone there besides the host, but I did my best to fit in.

A lot of the college girls around campus were dressed up, and they had their faces "beat" with stylish makeup. Some of them even wore heels on campus, and the ones at the party were no different. I was shocked by this trend, because I didn't dress up unless I was at bar or church. These girls got dressed up just to go to the library. We chilled for a while then started to play a game. I didn't want to participate at first, but the host was pressuring me to engage with the crowd. So, I did as I was told. Each person had to write a question down anonymously, and everyone would go around and answer it. I, of course, had to be the odd ball out the group and go the intellectual route instead of the sexual route. I can't remember what the question was, but once it was read, everyone looked around the room and the boy who was reading the question asked who wrote it. I raised my hand and explained why I wrote the question, and that instantly sparked a big debate. I felt like they respected me for asking such a debatable question. After that game, I felt that the party had run its course, so I said goodbye to everyone and went home.

A few days later, the host called me back over, except this time it was during the day. We made our way back to his bedroom and stayed in his room and watched television. I asked him about his parents, and he showed me a picture of a white couple. Apparently they had adopted him, and he was no different from me. Well, the dentist and his family didn't adopt me legally, but I felt like I was one of his kids. I just looked at the picture, nodded, and put it back on his night stand. I didn't want to make him feel uncomfortable by asking him anymore questions about his life. I laid on his bed and we cuddled and watched TV. As we talked, he leaned in slowly and started kissing me. I kissed him back. His roommate had come home, and I didn't feel comfortable having sex with another person in the house. I am not sure why, because in the past I had sex with a guy while laying right next to his best friend who watching TV. I have also been in a room full of people giving oral sex and almost had a threesome with two guys. I have definitely been in worse predicaments, but for some reason, I was uncomfortable with going all the way and settled to perform oral sex. I swallowed the semen when he ejaculated. Swallowing was the easiest thing for me to do, because I had a hard time looking at semen since it resembled spit and I would gag at the sight of it. I gagged when I had to swallow it, but I would rather just swallow it and get it over with. I guess he was satisfied with that, because I only heard from him one other time, and he was very distant and short. The next time I saw him was at graduation. He spoke, and I nodded and ran off to my place in line to walk across the stage.

I invited Mother, grandmother, my father and his wife, my old roommate, and my best friend and her sister to my graduation. Since the dentist graduated from the same school, he and his wife also came. By this time, their children either lived in different states or still attended college. I graduated in December 2009. I didn't have the grade point average that I wanted, but I was officially the first college graduate of my family. I moved back home, and I was ready to begin my job hunt. I thought my life was on the uphill slope, but I was sadly mistaken. The real test was about to begin and in no way was I prepared.

Chapter 10 – The Juggler

After graduation, I moved to Mother's house. She had upgraded from her small apartment to a duplex that had plenty of room. Although Mother was still relying on government assistance to survive, her moving into a new location with much more space had her in a better place. She lived directly across the street from my grandmother, so the family togetherness was in sync. A few months after living with Mother and job hunting, my Mother got a phone call that her landlord was selling her complex and she was to vacate the premise in 30 days. Mother was devastated. She had lived there for over a year and finally found a place she could call home. The new landlord was not approving Section 8 housing, so Mother was the first to get the boot. It didn't just happen to Mother. My grandmother and the complex next door were all in the same predicament and had to vacate the premises within 60 to 90 days.

I hadn't found a career job yet, so since my grandmother had more time to find a new plan than Mother did, my sister, Mother, and I would have to stay with her. I refused to do so, because I knew there wouldn't be enough room. I acted immediately and looked for a place that I could afford based on a nursing home dietary aide part time salary. I was so thankful to still work at the nursing home. It gave me steady income when I didn't have a full time job. I found a small one bedroom apartment that was located inside a big house. The owner was really nice but the area was not. I didn't know the neighbor below me, but there was always a foul odor that came from downstairs, and I was always itchy when I went to bed or laid on my futon. I was still trying to sort my job and living situation out along with my love life. Since I had moved back home, the partying every night at the bar was back in full swing. I started hanging with my best friend's sister a lot. She had golden skin and long hair that stopped right at her butt crack. She was called

Pocahontas a lot, because she reminded everyone of an Indian. She had the boys at her feet left and right, but she always managed to date men who were physically and verbally abusive to her. I never understood her choice in men, or why a woman as attractive as she would tolerate that behavior. I knew I never dated the best guys, but I was never attracted to men who physically abused me or called me derogatory names. It was never my cup of tea.

We went out to the bar together one night and came across an old fling my best friend had a one night stand with in the past. He was very tall and skinny and had long dreads. He was also a track runner. I thought he was an attractive guy, but I didn't look at him beyond being an attractive athlete. I was more interested in his friend who was also dark-skinned but had a bald head that was shaped like a milk dud. We never had sex, but we hung out once. I remember falling asleep on his lap and being very embarrassed when I woke up to notice that I had slobbered on his arm. We never kicked again after that.

My best friend's sister and I continued to kick it for the rest of the night. At the time my addiction was new phones, and the BBM (blackberry messenger) was the hot thing on the market back then. As I pulled out my phone and started to play around with the BBM, the tall guy with the dreads came over and started to talk to me. I thought nothing of it, because it was a harmless conversation.

He looked over and said, "Oh, you have a BBM, too. What's your pin code?"

I told him, and he quickly replied, "Do you know anyone else's code?"

Of course I knew he had sex with my best friend, so I hurried to the back and called her for permission to give her pin code to her old fling. With glee she agreed and asked me to hook her up with him. When I hung up and walked back to original post, he asked me again "Did you find some more people that I would know?"

I told him my best friend had a pin code and that's the only person in my friends list that we mutually know.

To my surprise, he disregarded my suggestion and asked, "Is there anyone else?"

I chuckled awkwardly, because I didn't know how I was going to explain that her old flame turned down the advance. After that her sister and I left the club, and I unexpectedly got a message through my BBM. It was a very simple message. It was a smiley face from the tall guy with the long dreads. I disregarded his smiley face, because I knew he worked in the social work field, so I asked if he had any leads for employment. He informed me that they were hiring at his job, and he told me to deliver my resume to his house or to one of his softball games. I was desperate for a full time job, and even though I thought it was unusual to give him my resume at his softball game, I overlooked it because I needed a job. Before ending our conversation, he mentioned how I was dancing the night at the club. I immediately shut it down and replied that I wasn't interested since he had already had sex with my best friend. I didn't believe in sharing penises with friends.

While getting him off my back, two of my old flames stumbled back into the picture. In addition, I was still sexually active with a boy I met at a club a few years back. This was around the time the news was blowing up about the Virginia Tech shooting. He and I had been sleeping together for three years, and he was moving out of town soon, so I wanted to hang on as long as I could. He was an engineer and the ladies loved him. He was very attractive and very short, but his sex game was out of control. I wanted to be with him at some point, but we had a big blow out when he told me he didn't want a girlfriend and wasn't making any commitment to anyone. I was heartbroken over him, but I got it over, and we were back to being buddies. Fuck buddies.

The first blast from the past was the boy who took my virginity. He sent me a request on Facebook, and I was so shocked that I literally had to call all my friends. I didn't know whether to accept it or not since we hadn't spoken or seen each other in ten years. I sent him a Facebook message and asked if he remembered me.

"Of course I do. We used to kick it, but your mom found out and threatened to all the police, so I got scared and left. You hated me after that, but I didn't want to go to jail. I had already been arrested before, and I wasn't trying to go back."

After I read that, I finally got to the real reason why we stopped talking. Our "breakup" was tough for me, because he just left without any explanation. On top of that, he embarrassed me in the hallways at school when he called me a bitch in front of everyone. Although I hadn't seen him in so long, I knew he had a kid because I worked with his baby's mama's sister at the restaurant, and she announced she was going to be an aunt. He proceeded to tell me that he was just concentrating on raising his son and offered to take me out on a date. I was open to the kind gesture, but I didn't know what to expect. My friends were very worried about this reunion between us based on how it ended so badly the first time, but I was willing to give it another chance. He took me bowling with his old high school friends who he always smoked and drank with regularly. They all remembered me and asked how I was doing. I caught them up on my recent achievement of graduating from college and working. The only thing they remembered about me was that I was a beast on the track in high school.

He lived with his mother who was a dog breeder, so when I went to the house, it smelled like dog shit. There were at least twenty dogs huddled in one area of the house, and they barked non-stop when there was a stranger in the home. His parents just so happened to be in Florida for two weeks, so I went to visit him every night. He made breakfast for me every morning, and we had sex after two weeks. It was a little different from the first time we had sex. This time I was experienced and had encountered bigger penises, so the pain and the bleeding was not included. Because he worked a landscaping job at the time and wanted to be the next Eminem, our time spent together became limited. His visitation with this son was a week at time, and when he wasn't with his son, he was at the studio laying down tracks or smoking and drinking with his friends. I wouldn't talk to him every day and I'd only see him once a month. Our non-relationship reunion grew old, so I eventually started to slip into the arms of the tall guy with the long dreads.

He had been contacting me every day on BBM the whole time I was hanging out with my first. One night while being fed up from being ignored, I went to his home. Although he'd slept with my best friend, I needed to know why he was so infatuated with me. He was cooking French fries and decided to share with me. As we began to talk I asked him what he wanted.

"I want to have sex with you."

He was so forward with me, and I wasn't used it. Most guys would lie, but he wasn't about those games. I reminded him that he and my best friend had sex.

With irritation in his voice, he replied, "I had sex with her one time. She played me, so it is what it is."

I was still skeptical, but he was giving me the attention I liked and deserved. As I sat for a moment in silence, I could see him getting hard.

I asked, "Um, what are you doing?"

With the biggest smile on his face, he said, "You turn me on."

He proceeded to pull it out and it was as long as a 20oz pop bottle and really thick. My eyes lit up like a Christmas tree, and I started to feel a throbbing sensation in my genital area. He must have just gotten out of the shower because it was ashy white, but that didn't stop me from licking the tip of it. Once that happened, I popped up and said I needed to speak with my best friend and if she felt uncomfortable with us hanging out, he had to stop contacting me. He agreed to the terms.

Unfortunately, it was never the right time to talk to my best friend. The first week I tried, she lost her job. The next week, her dad had just received the news to be sent off to Afghanistan, and the following week she and her sister got into a huge fight about her sister dating a guy she previously dated. This wasn't the first time they had been through that. They have dated each other's exes in the past, and it has driven their relationship into the ground. I couldn't imagine my sister or me dating the same man that either of us slept with or fell in love with at some point. I saw how their relationship became toxic and broken over the years, and I vowed to myself I would never do that to my friends nor my family members. However, that was clearly a lie. I had already broken girl code and had to come clean of my distasteful decision. I had feelings for my best friend's one night stand.

She was already so mad about her sister dating someone from her past, so I figured I'd add salt to the injury. I could tell she wasn't feeling what I had to say, but at the end of the conversation, she gave the green light. I clicked over and called him but was not sure about the decision because I didn't want our friendship to end. He told me not worry and pointed out that she should be grateful that she had a friend who would tell her, because most friends would sneak behind their friend's back and do it anyway. I understood what he was saying, but it still didn't feel right. I quickly shook the feeling of guilt and turned to my own selfish desires. I started having sex with him whenever I was not able to see my first. I just wanted to be sexually satisfied and I wanted attention.

To add to my black book list, the other old flame who decided to pop back up was the cute boy from my chemistry and math class who was not allowed to date outside his race. We hadn't talked in three years, but my friend saw him regularly since he started working at the hospital with her. She called and told me how he'd asked how I was doing and wanted me to call him sometime. I was confused with this request since the last time we spoke he didn't want a relationship because his last serious girlfriend had cheated on him. Plus, he was away at school, and he didn't want to do a long distance relationship. I remember I was so mad that I deleted his number and vowed to never talk to him ever again. Well, my mind quickly changed, and I asked my girlfriend to get his number for me. Just like that, we immediately picked up where we left off.

So, there I was juggling four guys at once. One was moving away which narrowed it down to three. Of the remaining three, I made the boy who took my virginity my boyfriend by the middle of June. I had to be honest and tell the dread head and the other boy that I had a boyfriend, but they didn't care. As long as I kept having sex with them, my boyfriend was not their concern. Half of the time, he wasn't my concern either. The relationship only lasted for two months, but I was heartbroken over his inability to put me first. I felt that I really loved him despite me having sex with two to three other men. When things ended between us, I just continued on with my foolishness. I was longing to be loved again, and the quickest way for me to feel loved was by taking off my clothes.

I did, however, gain some self-control when I landed an interview with the place I always wanted to work. The Job and Family Services building held my dream job. I knew I wanted to be a social worker to help others the way the dentist and his family made a difference in my life. I interviewed with two women - one with blonde hair and glasses and the other with a short bob hair style. I was nervous during the interview, but I landed the job. I needed guaranteed money and working at the mental health facility was not a full time position. On top of that, if I didn't have appointments scheduled, I didn't get paid. After working there for six months, I quit two weeks after the new job offer, and started working as an entry level county employee.

I was still bummed about my heart break, but I noticed that someone already had their eye on me on the first day of orientation. He also had a bald head that resembled a milk dud. He sat three people across from me at his computer. Every now and then I would catch him staring at me, and I knew I had him. Every time we had our breaks, we would make small talk. He even started to sit with me during lunch time. It was a good thing that we had lunch conversations, because I found that he had two kids. I knew I wasn't looking for anything serious, so his daddy daycare responsibilities had nothing to do with me or my plan. I knew it wasn't going to be long before I convinced him to come over. Ironically, I never found him to be attractive, but he was very nice though.

I invited him over one day after work. It was a bold move, but I assumed he did not have violent behaviors - at least that's not the vibe I got. Lucky for me he wasn't a violent person at all. When he knocked on the door, I greeted him in lingerie.

He had a grin on his face and exclaimed, "Oh my God! I have never been greeted at the door like this."

I smiled back and then removed his jacket as he entered my home and I walked him back to my room. It was quite snowy outside, which was the perfect scene for my burning desire. We began to kiss as I fell back on the bed and removed my thong panties. He removed his Mr. Roger's sweater, pants, and shoes. I could see that he had chest hair, and it was a huge turnoff for me, but I proceeded anyway. He put on the condom and climbed on top of me. He immediately put my legs behind his head and started pounding away. I kept my eyes clothes as long as I could, but when I finally did open them, he was staring right at me. This was extremely awkward, and he even leaned down to kiss me. The kiss caught me off guard, so I wasn't able to turn my head fast enough. A few seconds later, I could feel myself become dry from his pounding, chest hair, and his unexpected kiss. I pushed him off as soon as he climaxed, and I turned on the light and sat on my bed waiting for him to exit. He was very sweaty and slowing getting dressed. He tried to make conversation, but I responded with short answers. We had to work the next day, so I was ready to get in the shower and go to bed. He finally left, and I felt relieved. I accomplished my mission with no regard for someone else's feelings. I was a monster.

He tried to ask me out to the movies once after our one night stand. I was straightforward and told him I didn't want to go. I didn't see us going anywhere together, and he caught the hint.

Later while we were in a conversation at work, he stated, "I knew that I liked you. If you would have asked me last week if we were going to have sex, I would have said no."

I genuinely didn't know he had any feelings for me. I just wanted to satisfy my sexual desire, and I figured he would have caught on to that. Sadly for him, he was not aware that I had just gotten my heart broken, so I was the devil in disguise. I eventually told him about the recent heartbreak and how I wasn't ready to be with anyone else at the moment. He must not have taken it too well, because he didn't speak to me anymore until I bid to transfer to the Children Services Department. We would no longer be in the same building, so when he found out I was bidding to transfer he sent me a text.

Him: *You're trying to going to the other building?*

Me: *Yes, I always wanted to be social worker so I took the opportunity.*

Weeks before the announcement of my transfer, our boss pulled us all into her office and informed us that the company was going to start laying people off. She suggested that we bid on a position in the Children Services Division if we wanted a chance to stay with the company. I took my chances and got selected. He and I eventually got back on speaking terms right before my transfer. He finally got over being played by me and went back to the mother of his children. He proposed to her and they had another baby. A baby and marriage was the furthest thing from my mind. I was ready to start my journey as a soon to be social worker.

I had to start in one of the lowest positions in that department. I scanned records into the scanning system and rotated front desk duty weekly with two other women. We had a cool supervisor, but I was patiently waiting for my probationary period to be up so I could apply for a social worker position. It didn't come soon enough, and more rumors began to circulate about the company making layoffs to the support and clerical staff. The ones with the least seniority would be the first to go, and I knew I was on the chopping block. The other two ladies had been in the company for over fifteen years, so they were safe. I had cut off all the men that I was sleeping with, so my love life was at a standstill, and now my money was in jeopardy. I didn't know what I was going to do. I started looking for other social worker jobs but all of them required licensure. I called the board of Ohio and asked what I could do since I did not have a license. Basically, I was shit out of luck unless I went back to school for a Master's degree. I wasn't ready to go back to school nor was I ready to go full-time at the nursing home. I hated the hours, and I hated the director with his anti-social ass. Unfortunately, I was laid off. I had already called my supervisor at the nursing home and gave her a heads up a week prior to the lay-off. Lucky for me, a full-time position had just opened up, so I was able to go keep a steady flow of income until I figured out my next plan.

The lay-off left me feeling heartbroken. I couldn't find a job in the social work field. When I did have an interview, either I didn't have enough experience, or I didn't have a license. The nursing home was all I had to hold on to, so I at least had to be thankful for that. Even though I didn't want to go back to school, I had to if I wanted to be hired as a social worker. I buckled down and emailed the Director of Social Work at one of the top schools for social work in Ohio. He responded by telling me that because my undergraduate degree was not in social work, I had to attend school for an additional two years to receive my bachelors in social work. After that, I would have to apply to their master's program. I thought that was ludicrous, and I wanted to jump through that email and shake his ass while yelling, *I ALREADY HAVE A FOUR YEAR DEGREE IN A RELATED FIELD! DOESN'T THAT ACCOUNT FOR ANYTHING*? Too bad it didn't, and I had to accept my losses.

I didn't give up on my goal. As I sat weighing my options, I remembered being told that I was qualified to apply for the social worker assistant license when I called the board of social work. I didn't know what that was nor did I know who was hiring social worker assistants. I figured it wouldn't hurt to have the licensure, so I applied and a month later became a registered social worker assistant. In the spring of 2012, I ended up applying to the school where the director said I'd have to attend school for an additional two years. I was not happy about it, but I had to make the sacrifice in order to get a decent job in my field of choice. I still didn't know what I was going to do with the social worker assistant license. I wasn't eligible to be a social worker at the nursing home, because they required a license, therefore I was back on the job hunt. I figured I wouldn't be able to get a job in my hometown, so I ventured out.

During my hometown job search, I came across a posting at a child welfare agency located fifteen to twenty minutes away from my apartment. Although the candidate for the position posted had to be social worker with a licensure, I took the risk anyway. I figured the worse that could happen was to be told no. Since I had already failed miserably at relationships and getting interviews, I would just add this rejection to the pile. My decisions with men were not getting any better. I had started having sex with a Portuguese man. He wasn't attractive and he had a child and lived in his mother's home. She lived out of state for ten months of the year, because she was a full time caregiver to a filthy rich couple. I wasn't his type. He was used to dating Caucasian women and stated that "all black women had attitudes." I didn't care what he thought. He sold drugs for a living, so his nerve to stereotype me was shrugged off. I knew I was better than him on my worst day and had more to bring the table than just an attitude.

I was trying hard not to have sex with him, and I wanted to take things slowly. I failed after our second date. I was in a bitter place and I didn't trust anyone. I discovered a month before that my ex who I tried to rekindle the flame with, had started seeing another girl all while telling me that he thought of me a lot and cared about me but couldn't give me what I deserved. I didn't know what I deserved. I just wanted him to know that I loved him and was willing to ride or die to prove my love if needed. I was starting to think that getting a bachelor degree and living on my own without kids was becoming a curse. I also started to think men thought I was a hoe if I gave it up too soon. It's just that the more I tried to keep my legs closed, the more temptation crept up on me and slapped me right in the face.

The Portuguese man was very degrading to women. He didn't even respect his own mama. I know this because he invited me over while she was home for a visit. She quickly asked me to leave because I was in her house. I was already leery about visiting while she was home, so I asked if it was okay for me to come over and he insisted she wouldn't care and that he was "grown." However, it was clear that mama put her foot down and was not going to argue. After that incident, I later checked his Facebook page and noticed a new woman who was dark-skinned like myself lurking around on his page. She was too friendly which made me suspicious. A week later, I picked a fight with him, and he called me crazy. We didn't talk for two weeks until he eventually made his way back to my house, and we had make up sex. I asked him if he had slept with her, and he admitted that he had and he was going to see her because she thought he was the father of her four year old daughter. I was floored by his honesty yet disgusted by his actions. Who was I to talk? I was no better, but he didn't know. I continued to have sex with him, but we abruptly ended things due to his lack of respect for women. We got into a text message war, and my last response to him before I blocked his number was "Go Die."

The child welfare agency I randomly sent my resume to finally contacted me to fill out an application and schedule an interview. That was the first good news I had received in a long time. The lady on the phone told me I wasn't qualified for the social worker position because I didn't have a license, but there was a social worker assistant position available with the hours of noon to eight. That was right up my alley. I hated mornings, and I was sick of the nursing home and their drama. I didn't hear from them right away, but I finally got a call to schedule an interview. I was nervous, but I held my head up and got refocused. Since I was in school, I received a refund check from my student loans and planned a trip to go to the Super bowl festivities in Indiana. I needed a break from everything and everyone, but I had to knock this interview out before I went. I wore a black blazer, a dark gray skirt, and a printed shirt. The interview was long, but it was worth the wait. I didn't know anyone up there, so I had no connections. All I had was my personality and the grace of God. He knew I needed this. Everyone knew I needed this.

After the interview, we drove five hours to get to Indiana. I was so excited to be on a mini vacation. I went with my best friend's sister and a woman that I worked with at the nursing home. She very quiet and her skin tone was "high-yellow." We didn't really speak much when I first met her, because her quietness made me feel like she didn't want any parts of my crazy personality. She seemed very mature. I served residents in the dining room where her office was located. I would hear her gospel music playing as I cleaned the tables, so I knew she was a woman of God. She would come through our cafeteria line and the other lunch ladies and I would turn our noses up because she didn't seem to be friendly. Of course I had a change of heart, and thought to myself, *I have never done anything to this woman, so there is no need for her not to like me.* I decided to speak to her and to my surprise, she spoke back. After that, she saw me cleaning tables near her office after the residents were finished eating. This time she spoke first. From that moment on, she started to open up and asked for random things located in the cupboards of our kitchenette.

We eventually became friends, and I got to know the reason behind her quietness. Come to find out, she had a son and she was a divorcee. She lost custody of her son to her ex-husband who was a principal at my old high school. He made her pay him child support. What a jerk right? After talking to her more, I later found out that her husband was verbally abusive and cheated on her with my best friend and her sister's cousin. This did not come out until we were on our way to Indiana. I told her the name of my best friend's sister and she asked, "What's her cousin's name?" Once I verified the names, it was confirmed that her husband had an affair with someone I knew. Small world.

That didn't stop us from going to Indiana. When we arrived, there were thousands of people in the downtown area ready for some football. Although I am more of a basketball fan, I was just ready to experience something new. I had only been on a plane once, which was the most terrifying experience ever, and had only lived in one other city besides my hometown. This road trip to Indiana was another item crossed of my bucket list. I was branching out and proud of myself for doing so. The dentist always told me I needed to broaden my horizons, and that's exactly what I was doing. As we were getting off the charter bus to explore the city, I received a phone call.

"Hello?" I said confused, because I didn't recognize the number. "Keshia, we would like for you to take a drug test. I can't officially offer you the position because our Executive director is not here, but I'd like to get a few things out of the way. Here is a list of places where you can go to take the drug test. Once you have done that, they will send us the results."

"Of course, I can get that done next week," I replied with such excitement.

My best friend's sister and my nursing home friend couldn't wait for me to hang up before asking me did I get the job. I told them I had to take a drug test first, but with confidence they said, "You got it!"

The rest of the weekend went smoothly. We saw LL Cool J and rapper Meek Mill perform at a night club. We visited a soul food restaurant where celebrities frequented, and I was able to take a picture with one of the members from P. Diddy's former band, Day 26. I couldn't remember his name, but he always wore the jherri curl. Madonna also performed that year, and her dancers stayed at our hotel. I took a picture with them, too. They looked really young, and they were beautiful. If I didn't become a social worker, I would have gone to school for dance. I was too scared to pursue my dreams at that time. I knew if I wanted to be the best dancer, I would have to attend a performing arts school out of state and I was too chicken at the age of eighteen. The ladies and I enjoyed our mini vacation and the Super Bowl festivities.

I got back home and completed my drug test. I knew I would pass it, but I was still nervous. I waited around all week to hear back from the hiring manager, but received an unexpected phone call instead. The agency who laid me off decided they wanted me back and implied that I should apply for a social worker position. I was at a loss for words before I told the lady on the phone that I had already had an interview and completed a drug screen for the other agency. I told her they were awaiting the results and the Executive Director to return before officially offering the position. I let her know that I would call them back a week later with my decision.

I didn't want to be a bother to the new agency, but I had no other choice than to rush the decision. When I called the HR lady who told me to complete a drug test, she stated that although she couldn't officially offer the position without the signature of the Executive Director, I should call the other agency and tell them I would not be returning. I still wanted to wait for the official phone call to have the position offered to me, so I waited a couple days before calling the other agency back. After another day or so of waiting, I received a phone call from the HR lady.

When I answered, she said, "Hi, Ikeshia. Now I can officially offer you the position. Are you still interested?"

"Yes I am," I replied, feeling relieved.

She then began to go over all of my benefits, which I was already familiar with from being a government employee, and she told me my hourly rate. It was a four dollar increase. You couldn't tell me God was not good. When she told me that, I didn't hear anything else. I wasn't going to struggle like Mother anymore. I was going to be able to pay my bills and finally start living the life I dreamed of since I was fifteen years old. I hung up the phone and called the other agency back to inform them that I would not be returning. Since it was the day before Valentines' Day and my boy toys were slim to none, the new job was a Valentine's Day gift to me.

Unfortunately, Betty had run her course. Her muffler was so loud that people could hear me coming a mile away. Her tires were so balled that I barely made it home when the snowstorms hit. I felt like she wasn't going to last driving back and forth to school twice a week and work every day. I had two options, either move closer to my new job or get a new car. Besides my first car in high school, I had never been to a car lot to purchase a car. I wasn't ready to make that step, so breaking my lease was my only option. I wasn't willing to take the chance of my car dying when I had just landed my dream job. Something had to go and it was apartment.

I had only been to the city where the agency was located for college parties. It was a college town, so I only knew how to get to the bars. I google mapped the distance between the agency and the first apartment I found. It was more than ten minutes away, therefore, I wasn't taking it. I eventually found a closer one. It was a little pricey, but I could afford it since I was making more money. It had a spiral staircase, garage, dishwasher, 1.5 bathrooms and two bedrooms. They were running a special, so I was very happy to pay the inexpensive deposit, and I jumped head first into signing my lease. I was going to be away from my friends, but this wasn't the first time I had moved away. Plus, I was still going to keep the nursing home job. It was extra income and my backup plan. I didn't have any boys, so this was my chance to start over. School was going well, and I was getting all As. Although the job was demanding, I was learning new things every day. I was finally in a good spot until he came along.

I knew him from high school. He was attractive back in the day but unfortunately had a baby with his long-time girlfriend at the age of fifteen. He dropped out of school and joined the Armed Forces. I hadn't seen him since high school, and the only connection we had was on Facebook. He knew I liked the vanilla men, so he decided to send me a message. He immediately disclosed that he loved black women and the last woman he was with was a black woman. He told me they were engaged and she was pregnant with his child before losing it after three months. I knew he liked the chocolate, but I didn't know he was that deep in since the mother of his child was white. While we were sending messages back and forth, I took it upon myself to snoop through his pictures. He looked very different from high school, and he had gained quite a bit of weight. He wasn't as attractive as he used to be, but he liked the chocolate girls, so that's all that mattered. He offered to give me his number, and I figured it wouldn't hurt to take it. My list of boys was long gone. It was close to Valentine's Day again, so I was open to anybody at this point. The problem was he lived in another state.

We talked for about a month before he started to bring up marriage. He began to send me pictures of rings, and he shipped all my gifts to my townhouse a week before Valentine's Day. He even bought me a pair of shoes to go with the gifts. It's been said that diamonds are a girl's best friend, but I beg to differ. He sent flowers and expensive makeup and perfume. I was so taken aback by all the money he'd spent in such a short time frame that I started to feel good. He even offered to pay for my school tuition if I would move to his next base with him. It sounded like a good offer and his priorities were all in order, but I just wasn't quite ready to make that step. We continued to see each other virtually until one day he planned to drive twelve hours to see me. We hadn't seen each other physically since high school, and that was ten years ago. I was nervous but excited to see the guy who wanted to make me his wife.

I was also in the process of moving again. I wanted to move back home since I had bought a new used car. Her name was Bernice. She was a burgundy Impala. I had broken my sectional six months prior during a three month fling with a skinny white boy who reminded me of James Dean. His hair was slick back on the side while the rest stood straight up. Although he worked jobs here and there, he was a lost soul. He never wanted better for himself, and no matter how much I tried, his marijuana use and not wanting to be in a relationship ultimately made me move on with my life. I didn't want to but I had to keep it moving. Anyway, I needed furniture before moving into my new place, so the army guy and Mother who had received her tax money at the time, both went half on my furniture. I found it online from an old couple. They only charged me $300 for a couch, loveseat, and recliner. Can we say winning?

After years of being misused by guys, I started to realize I was worth more than just a cheap dinner date. A dude was going all out for me and he was even going to travel twelve hours across several states to see me. I had never had this happen before, and although he wanted to move a lot faster than I did, I was worthy of a good man. It was unfortunate that after his three day visit, I was not only turned off by his sexual performance, but he wasn't as attractive in person nor was he emotionally stable. His true colors started to show. He didn't like the fact that I went out to the bar all the time. I didn't see the issue. I was doing it before he came along, and I didn't plan on slowing down anytime soon. Everything was awkward and I knew right then and there that I would never marry him. We kept in contact after I moved into my new place. He had moved to his new base in Hawaii, and I was seeking out graduate programs to elevate my career. I told him I would fly to Hawaii, but once I found out that I would be the one paying for majority of my ticket which was a thousand dollars, I backed up from that idea. I had a new car (well sort of) and moved into a house where I had more than just electric to pay without a roommate. Any extra money I had was not going toward a plane ticket for a relationship that was at dead end stop.

I had bigger and better things to do. I had to find a graduate program who was going to accept me. Everyone at my job had their master's degree and/or their license to be a social worker. I felt like a kid and I felt others treated me that way because I looked young and I wasn't on their professional level. I wanted more. I was the first college graduate from my family, but I didn't want to stop there. I was determined to keep moving forward. I still worked at the nursing home, so I was still able to get extra income. I wasn't giving up on that job even if someone begged me to do it. I told myself that I would never be like Mother, no matter the cost. If I had to work twelve jobs to make ends meet, that's what I was going to do.

I applied to my first graduate program. I knew two years before when I emailed the director of social work that I wasn't going to be accepted because I still didn't have my undergraduate degree in social work. After I completed my first semester in their undergraduate social work program, I realized that something wasn't right. If other people were accepted into the graduate social work program with non-social work undergraduate degrees while I had one in a related field, then why couldn't I be accepted? Why did I have to have an undergraduate in social work first? I knew my competition would be tough, but not that tough. Needless to say they didn't accept me, and I was devastated. I was so hurt that I met my male best friend, who people called Mr. Cooper at the bar and cried in his arms.

Mr. Cooper and I had known each other for ten years. He worked at the nursing home with me. After we had given each other the stare down for a few months after he was hired, we finally broke down and started talking. He was a rich black kid who grew up without his father as well. His mother worked herself to death to become a successful business owner, so even though his father wasn't present, he never had to struggle like Mother and I did. He had a sibling who was his exact opposite. He always was getting into trouble with the law and never respected the fact that his mother worked hard to give them a plush lifestyle. They were so opposite, but luckily for me, Mr. Cooper wanted more out of life like I did and understood my struggles. I could count on him for anything, and he would come through for me.

Many people didn't understand our relationship for many reasons. Number one, we are opposite sexes, so the idea of us just being friends was hard for people to believe. We both had direct personalities. Most would call it aggressive, but I would rather use the term direct. We spoke the truth no matter how another person felt - that's if that person wanted to hear our opinions. We fought against each other and fought for each other. Normally, two direct personalities end up clashing, and sometimes we didn't see eye to eye on different topics, but we remained truthful no matter what the situation was. When it came to us defending each other against an outsider, people knew we were the epitome of a ride or die relationship. He had my back, and I had his. When he saw how hurt I was about not being accepted into the program, he told me to not give up and reminded me that everything happens for reason. He assured me that I was going to be okay and that everything was going to work itself out. He was right.

Chapter 11 – Woman

A few months later, a recruiter from one of the top schools for social work in the nation was coming to the agency to speak to a group of employees whose desire was to further their education. I was very hopeful that this meeting would go well. One of the perks was that they offered an intensive weekend program which only required school attendance one weekend a month. The other perks were the program was designed for minorities and employees of a county agency. The odds of me being accepted were looking good. The only downfall was the cost. One year at their school totaled more than my undergraduate degree that took me five years to get. It was either all or nothing, and this was my last shot. I didn't want to go to school for another three years, but I knew the only way to move forward was to apply. I was financially stable, but I wasn't sure how I was going to manage for another three years having to stay in a hotel once a month while attending school. In addition, traveling an hour away to go to school would eventually run my car into the ground more, since I already drove a half hour to work. I couldn't just think of all the cons, I had to take the risk and do it. Besides, with a school like that on my resume, I was guaranteed to get a good job right? At least that's what my mentality was.

I had to fill out so many forms and find three references. Two of my references were females, one was my supervisor and the other was an older black lady in my unit who had also attended the same school. She wore an afro and always kept it real. She let me in on the scoop that the expensive college I was applying to wasn't diverse back in the day but things had changed since then. She had already worked in a prison for twenty years, so this was her recreational job. I was not sure why she chose child welfare as a recreation, but if the stress and anxiety was worth it, then so be it. The last reference I had to get was not from a person that I was typically expecting, but I somehow backslid into my old ways.

We met when I first got hired at the agency. Another coworker introduced me to him, and after we greeted each other, he stared at me for another minute or two. I could see him out the corner of my eye, but I didn't want to startle him out of his gaze. I didn't see him again for another few weeks after that. We were out in the lobby area, and unfortunately I had been at the agency for quite some time, but a random employee didn't recognize me. I had to set her straight that I was in fact an employee. Maybe it was the sundress I was wearing coupled with my side ponytail that made her think I was a client. He was standing on the other side of her, and after I stated that I was an employee, he reached across her and introduced himself. Again. We shook hands, and then I quickly walked away to supervise some kids in our children's room.

Each time we saw each other, we would stare at each other a little longer than the time before. He had intense blue eyes and white hair. He was probably the most attractive older man I had ever seen. I knew he was interested in me, but I also saw his wedding ring on his finger, so I wasn't going to get very far. Our quick hellos turned into conversations and eventually had me making a trip to his office every day. He complimented me on how I looked and made hints on how much he wanted me. He had two kids, and I knew I would be the whore of the century if I took him up on his advances. I didn't see it that way though, since I wasn't the one who made the vow to get married, he did. However, if anyone found out, I knew they would blame me. I had slept with a married man before, except I didn't know he was married until a year after we had sex. Hell, I didn't even know he had kids until three months of us having sex. I eventually met the wife, and she was already with someone else. We even became social media friends. That's when Myspace was the place to be. He told me they got married to get more welfare benefits, because he had just gotten out the joint. Plus, he was thirsty for pussy, and she was the first one available. It just so happened that she got pregnant not once, not twice, but three times. Still, according to him, no love existed in their relationship.

Back to my dilemma, married or not, I needed that final reference. If that meant I had to have sex to get it, then that's what it had to be. I felt he was doing me a favor by agreeing to my request, so I was preparing myself to break up another happy home. Unfortunately, the population at the agency was 90% female and the old hags were out to get the young, successful tenderonis like myself. They started to notice my frequent visits to his office, and one of them was bold enough to ask him what was going on between us. When I found that out, I immediately stopped all communication. If I saw him in the hallways, I would put my head down as if he didn't exist. If we did make eye contact, I would simply nod my head. I was very fortunate that he had already turned my reference letter in to the school, so I didn't have to worry about scrambling to find another one. I eventually found out who the person was who was all up in our business. I was mad at first, but that quickly turned into confusion. I didn't understand how what I did with my pussy was anyone else's business. Yes, he was a married man, but if there was going to be a mess, I would handle it. How bad could it get? I felt I had already been through the worse, therefore I could handle anything.

A couple months later, I received an email with an acceptance letter to one of the top universities in the nation. I didn't know what to say or who to call first. My eyes filled with tears of joy, and I couldn't believe I was going to get my master's degree in social work. I didn't think about the cost or how much time I had to invest for the next three years. All I cared about was making it happen at whatever cost, and I did. Once I finally gained control of my emotions, I called Mr. Cooper and then called my family. They were so happy for me and couldn't wait to celebrate. Anytime we got big news whether good or bad, we celebrated it at the bar. I was not a big fan of drinking, so one drink was my max. If I had two or more drinks, they would have to carry me out, or I would stumble out of the bar. My tolerance for alcohol was very low, but that night I was willing to take my chances on more than one drink.

I googled the cheapest hotel fifteen minutes away from the school, and as soon as I found one, I used my GPS to get to the location. It wasn't the best hotel, but they served free breakfast and had a shower and bed, so I was good. When I got to orientation, I was nervous. I didn't know what to expect and was hoping I wasn't going to be too lost, considering I didn't have an undergraduate degree in social work. When I arrived, I noticed other black students showing up to orientation and the field director and instructor were also black. My old coworker was right, because they had clearly changed some things around at that school. I was actually ready to get started after we got through our two days of orientation. We didn't have to start our internship until the following spring semester, which gave me six months to figure out where I wanted to complete my internship. It didn't take me long to figure this out. I was able to do my internship at the same place I worked and get paid for it. It was an easy decision. There were some people who struggled to find an internship or hated where they were and had to change their internship placement. I was good to go, so I had no worries.

I was financially stable, since I received a refund from my loans. Books and a new laptop were checked off my list, and my bills were caught up. There were no men in my life, well not at the time. I started to grow close to a few girls at work since we had something in common. We were all single. They didn't know my childhood struggles, nor were they aware that I was insecure about my dark skin and big lips. They didn't know the only thing I thought I could offer a man was sex. I had reinvented myself, and I wanted to reinvent my dating life. I had been through all the heartbreaks in the world, at least I thought.

Figuratively, my guard was like a stone wall, but I was finally ready to bring it down and become a better woman. I figured since I was working on being a better woman, didn't I deserve a better man? The issue was that I never knew how to go about getting a better man. I looked back on all the fuckups I made and realized Mother never taught me how to have a relationship, and since my father wasn't around, he was no help either. I had no idea how to figure it out, so one of the girls at work had a suggestion.

"Keshia, how about online dating? I am doing it."

I was very against it at first, because I felt I was at an all-time desperation if I had to get online to find a man. I didn't consider her to be desperate, but online wasn't for me. I didn't know those men and nor could I see them unless we met in a public place. I would see the commercials for match.com on TV, where couples found their true love after joining for six months. They never advertised black women, so I didn't think I would have any luck. Well I was wrong. Sort of.

A few weeks later, I checked in with my coworker, and found out that she had met a guy. She was head over heels, and the glow on her face and her awesome date story had me curious. I went home that night and researched a dating website. It was free, so I couldn't beat it. I didn't know what to expect, since I wasn't even sure of how this was going to work. I uploaded my best selfies and tried to have an interesting yet positive profile. Within 48 hours, my inbox were flooded with messages. Some of the messages were good, and some were creepy. I could not believe how quickly I'd grabbed the attention of those men. I was so popular that I received a message from the creator that said: *Your profile has gotten a lot of views, making you one of the most attractive people on our site. Whatever you are doing, keep it up.* I wasn't doing anything besides uploading a few pictures and giving a snippet of my educational and social background. Apparently that's all men need to know to spark their interest. I went on a few dates, but after awkward conversations there were no second dates planned.

I met a white guy who was a correctional officer and seemed very appropriate. He worked for the county and that was a plus for me, since I did too. We exchanged messages for few days before we exchanged numbers. He was very serious about being in a relationship, through further conversation, I learned that he had a biracial daughter. It made me secure when a white guy either dated, married, or had biracial children by a black woman. I needed to know I wasn't their "first black woman" or some kind of sick fetish or bucket list item. I have been those things before, so I needed to check those few things off my list. I never had black men chase after me, not even make me their significant other. So, I stayed where I was celebrated, and it was with the white men. The correctional officer stayed near my school, so we met at a restaurant down the street from my hotel the next time I was in town for school. My classmates, who were also other black women, were a little nervous about me meeting someone I'd met online. They made me write down his name and number just in case I didn't return. I was sure I wouldn't get kidnapped, but it was better safe than sorry. When he arrived, he had flowers and a Hello Kitty stuffed animal. I was very much pleased, but something didn't look right about his face. When he laughed, I noticed he kept covering his mouth. I finally figured out that he had a huge gap between his teeth. Although gaps are not attractive to me, I let it slide because he was very nice and the date went well.

We continued to talk for another couple of weeks after that, and he wanted to make our relationship official. It had only been a few weeks. I wasn't ready, but I agreed anyway. We made plans for him to come visit me at my home. I lived a little over an hour away from him, and the snow was making it hard for anyone to travel. That didn't stop him though. A few days before he came, I was venting to him about not having enough money to pay for something. I can't remember what it was, but I was crying and very upset. When he came to see me, he brought the $100 I needed along with a few more Hello Kitty stuffed animals and some chocolate. For whatever reason, things changed when I saw him the second time. I was no longer interested in him. He wanted to cuddle, and I didn't want him to touch me. I wanted nothing to do with him. I just wanted my money. We did eventually perform oral sex on each other that night, because my hormones were out of control. I believe Mother Nature was around the corner. She always made me either act devilish toward people or be the polar opposite and become overly emotional.

That night, I made him sleep on the couch while I slept in my recliner. By morning, I told him he could sleep in my bed, but he wanted me to join him. I didn't want to, but I did anyway. He started to kiss on me and asked me to get on top of him. I asked him why.

He replied, "Because I am horny."

I was literally disgusted, but I climbed on top anyway. While I was going up and down, he was staring right into my eyes. I tried to keep my eyes closed. Suddenly, he rolled me over and climbed on top of me, and without taking off his shorts or shirt, he stuck it in and started pounding me. While he continued to stare into my eyes, I quickly shut them and had a flashback of the last guy I had sex with that I didn't care about. It the worse position to be in for those few moments. All I wanted was for him to stop and that's exactly what I made him do. I was not comfortable, and at that point I didn't care how he felt. I think he got the vibe that I wasn't into it or him. He left the next morning, and we were able to be honest with each other a few days later that it wasn't going to work out.

I moved on to another guy that I met online. He was an attractive redhead and seemed to be interested in me. He worked two jobs, and I enjoyed his company. We only went out on one date, and I was never invited to his house. He claimed to live with a gay couple that he'd found on Craigslist. It sounded suspicious to me, but I was never bothered because I had my own place, so we could see each other without interruptions whenever we wanted. I vowed to myself that I wouldn't have sex with anyone until I was in a serious relationship. He tried to make a move on me, but I was proud of myself for sticking to my guns. I was starting to catch on to the game. If a guy wasn't courting and only wanted to come to my place or make me come to his place, I knew he was only interested in one thing. He was eliminated quickly. We never saw or spoke to each other again. I was playing the good girl for a few months. I was keeping my legs clothes for once, but I still didn't give up hope on the online dating. I kept going on dates, but nothing was panning out. I figured it was because I wasn't giving it up fast like I used to do in the past. As my hope began to diminish, so did my will to keep my legs closed.

I came across one of my old enemies. He was a successful head basketball coach. He used to make fun of me back when I was in middle school because I was dark-skinned. We ran into each other at the bar, and boy was he finer than ever. I was wondering if he remembered how badly he had slaughtered my self-esteem. I am assuming he didn't, since we exchanged kind words. I even offered to give him my number, and he called that night. I went over to his house planning to just hang out. I wore a white dress with a flowered blazer over it. I didn't look my best, but I was presentable. Apparently, he liked it, because while we were sitting on his roommate's bed laughing and giggling, he reached over and grabbed my boob.

"Oh, these are pretty perky," he said pretending to be surprised.

At that moment, I knew things were going to go south. His roommate, his roommate's friend, my old enemy, and I laid across the bed. It was quite weird that four adults were laying in the bed together. He had his arm up above my head, and then he slowly reached down to turn my face toward him. We began to kiss, but stopped when we heard one of the others change sleeping positions. I was cool with kissing him, but I didn't plan for it to go any further. I started to get cold and the position I was laying in was starting to hurt, so I got up, put my shoes on, and walked toward the bedroom door.

As I was walking out, I heard, "Where are you going?"

I paused and then turned and said, "I think I'm just going to go home."

He quickly got up and followed me toward the front door, then said, "Well you don't have to go. We can just lay here on the couch."

I figured if we weren't laying in the bed and not sleeping in there with the other two in weird positions, we would be fine on the couch. Boy, was I wrong. He laid on top of me and put his hands under my dress. His eyes bulged out of his head when he figured out I didn't have on underwear. He gave a slight pause before he just stuck his fingers right inside my wet hole. I let out a soft moan because I hadn't had sex in close to five months. He didn't stop once he knew it felt good to me. After ten minutes of making out on the couch, he asked if I wanted to go upstairs since it wasn't very comfortable laying on the couch. I agreed. He had one of the biggest dicks I had ever seen for a white boy, and it was some of the best sex I had ever had. I made sure I went to church the next day with Mr. Cooper. He was hung over when we arrived church. When service was over, we both made it clear that we were the example of sex, drugs, and alcohol.

Right after the coach came another mistake with someone who wanted me so badly. I kept denying him for two to three months, but he was persistent. He had two kids, and I knew the mother of his children. He was a dog, and I knew of his cheating stories. I didn't know why he tried to catch me up in his web of lies and his tangle of torture, but he did. I liked that he chased me. I could dangle my pussy over his head like a piece of meat dangling over a dog. He was a dog, so I treated him like one. I didn't want to give it up to him, because I knew all his people and they knew me. Unfortunately, my devilish ways crept back in and I slipped. Hard. He lasted not even thirty seconds before I made him stop. It wasn't right, and I had to pull myself together before I ended up in a bigger mess. I had to move on quickly, so I went back to the online dating site where I found the surgeon.

He looked a little nerdy from his profile picture, but what more could I expect from a surgeon. I read through his profile and everything was perfect except one thing. His religion. He was an atheist. I came from a strong Christian background, and I even praise danced for a few years. All I knew growing up was if you didn't believe in God, you were the devil. Although his religion or lack thereof was a huge turnoff he excelled in every other area. Could I really judge him off of that one part of his life? Was he really a bad person just because he didn't believe in God? I didn't know the answer, but I was sure to find out.

We hit it off right away. We met at a local restaurant after I had gotten off of work one evening. I was so nervous, because I couldn't believe I was going out to eat with a surgeon - well soon to be surgeon. He was in his residency and had one more year to go. I admired his dedication to go to school for such an extended period of time. When I arrived, he saw me from our table. When I looked up and saw a random man pop up waving rapidly, I knew it was him. Although it was really dim in the restaurant, when I got closer he looked just like his pictures. I was hoping he found the same to be true for me.

The first thing he asked was, "Are those your eyelashes? I love them!"

I was more confused as to why he didn't ask were those my eyes because I was wearing hazel contacts, and if my hair was real because I was wearing a curly wig.

Apparently the only thing that caught his attention were my lashes. Although I had been wearing wigs for several years now, the whole wearing fake eyelashes was a new thing. I thought they brought out my eyes, which clearly they did since the surgeon noticed them. They weren't even the long ones, so he must've been paying very close attention.

After our great conversation and dinner, he walked me to my car and kissed me on the cheek right before I got in it to leave. I felt it was a successful date. Apparently he did too, since he sent me text that said: *It was really great hanging out with you. Hopefully we can see each other again.* Finally! I met someone on my level and even a bit higher who was interested enough to take me out on a date rather than back to his house or want to come back to mine. Besides his non-existent religion, he was okay in my book. We continued to go on a few more dates. I learned that he was originally from Nebraska, and his father was an ER physician. His father had his own private jet and flew to England whenever he wanted to see his girlfriend. His mother was a nurse, and his brother was a physician assistant. Everyone in his family had a medical background, and they were well established.

When it came to explaining what my parents did for a living, I had to swallow hard. Really hard. I had to tell him that Mother only worked as a cashier and father worked in a kitchen at a restaurant. At least that's the last I heard. I guess he was expecting to hear some extravagant story, since I worked two jobs and was pursing my masters. I also had to tell him that I moved out of my house and was staying at my nursing home supervisor's house. I wanted to save money while finishing school, and Mother's house wasn't an option since she had no room. My supervisor needed help with paying the bills because her ex-husband screwed her over on her taxes. We decided I would stay with her and her new husband to help them out. I didn't know how long I would be staying with her, but as long as I was saving money and had somewhere to sleep I was content. Plus, it would help keep my legs closed since I refused to bring a man to my supervisor's home. How embarrassing would that be?

She kept calling me one night while I was at dinner with him, and I had to answer.

"What do you want? I am at dinner."

Normally she would scream at me, and that day was no different.

"THERE'S A TORNADO WATCH. WHERE ARE YOU?"

I had to tell her that I was safe and would be home shortly after we finished eating. I didn't know what he was going to think when I told him I stayed with her, but he already had a confused on look on his face when I answered the phone and said it was my supervisor from work. After that, we continued to talk every few days. He tried to explain his schedule, but his rotation never made sense. I would just wait until he contacted me. He never tried to make a sexual pass at me which was nice, but when it's a week before Mother Nature arrives, I am like a cat in heat. It gets so bad that I could hump anything that was moving or not. It was a feeling and urge that I couldn't control, and I was ready for whatever the surgeon was bringing to table sexually.

For whatever reason, he also had me contact him on his google plus number. He claimed that while he worked in the hospital, he could not get reception. However, he was able to use his WIFI signal to receive texts, calls, and emails. One day while at work, I sent him a picture of me in a striped red sun dress with a jean jacket saying:

I want to come over tonight to see you.

He quickly responded with: *WOW, YOU LOOK ABSOLUTELY GORGEOUS!*

He then proceeded to tell me what time he got off and gave me his address for me to GPS it. I was in predator mode, and I was getting ready to catch my prey. I was ready and willing, and so was he. I figured it had been almost two months and we had been on more than three dates. He wasn't aggressive by any means and seemed like he was super interested. He had made a few comments before, but I disregarded them because I didn't want him to think I was "loose." Go figure.

I went to his one bedroom apartment. He drove a new Audi, so I'd assumed his apartment would match his car. It didn't. You got to save money somewhere, I guess. He walked me around his small apartment. The living room had a couch, loveseat, and a huge big screen TV. There was a bicycle parked behind the front door. Although he had an area for a dining room table, that space was occupied with a computer desk, a keyboard, and workout equipment. We went into the kitchen where he showed me his sink full of dishes, his outdated stove, and his refrigerator. At least he had plenty of food. It reminded me of when Mother would get her food stamps. We also had a kitchen full of random stuff. He briefly showed me the bathroom which was clean from what I saw. I can't stand a filthy bathroom. It's an instant turnoff. His bedroom was really boring. It was just a bed with a dresser. It was as cold as a jail cell.

I shouldn't have expected much interior design skills from him. Besides, I was only there for one thing, and it wasn't to evaluate how well he decorated his home. We went back to the living room and he sat down first. I laid down and put my head on his lap. He began talking and then his hands slipped inside my dress to caress my boobs. It felt so good to feel a man's touch. Once he saw that I liked his touch, he leaned down and kissed me, then slid his hands slowly between my legs. I was dripping wet like a faucet, and I could feel him getting hard. I made soft moans and he began to aggressively kiss me harder and harder. I quickly got up and took off my dress. He looked at me in a daze. I pulled off his shirt, then his shorts. He pulled down his underwear. He wasn't the biggest, but I could work with it. I got down on my knees in front of him and didn't hesitate to start sucking. He grabbed the back of my head as I went up and down slowly. He was moaning as if it was the best oral sex he had ever received.

When I paused to catch my breath, he pulled me up and said, "Lay back down on the couch."

I was a little nervous only because I knew what that meant. He slid down to the end of the couch by my feet and opened my legs. He took off his glasses and the tip of his tongue touched my "lips." He opened the lips and slid his tongue up and down. Although it was always an uncomfortable feeling, it felt good nonetheless. When he finished, I got up and grabbed his hand as I led him to the cold jail cell. We started to kiss once he laid me back on the bed.

He asked, "Do you want to?"

"Yes," I replied.

He leaned to the left to his bed and retrieved a condom from his night stand. He slipped the condom on then leaned back down and kissed me while he slowly slide it in. We both moaned as though it was the best sex we had ever had. To my surprise, the sex was good, and although two months was not a long time, for sex it's an eternity. When the night ended, we kissed goodnight and I went home. We only saw each other one other time after that because I got on my online profile and saw he was online. I immediately became suspicious, and I made it clear to him that I was interested in a relationship not just being a "fuck buddy." His response was less shitty than I thought it would be. He replied: *I don't have much time to do anything, let alone talk to anyone else, but I am trying to take this seriously.* I didn't know how to take that response, but it didn't give me the direct answer I wanted. A couple weeks later, he got the boot because I had finally met THE ONE.

Chapter 12 – The Captain

I had known him for the past ten years. We met through his ex-wife. He told other people we met through college, and although we did attend the same college, that's not how we met. We only had virtual contact with each other because we were Facebook friends. I had deactivated my account for a while, but when I reactivated it, his ex-wife sent me a message. I hadn't seen her in ten years. I wouldn't consider her a best friend, but she was an associate. Of course when we "caught up" on our lives, I asked her how she and her husband were doing. She admittedly said: *We are not together anymore. We grew apart. I have a baby by someone else.* I was floored by her confession. I would have never pictured them apart or divorced for that matter. Sadly she also confessed that she had a baby by a black guy who was a drug dealer who had four other kids with two other women. She said the sex was good, but it wasn't worth all the headache she was going through. He didn't help her financially, and he continued to see other women. It was a bad situation. I told her I was sorry for her and that she would be okay. I assured her that I would be there to support her if she needed me.

An hour later, I received a message from her ex-husband. He asked why I deactivated my Facebook account. My response was: *Well, because I needed a break. I am back now.* I didn't want to tell him that I knew that he and his ex-wife split, because I wasn't for sure if it was a sore subject for him to discuss. I quickly found out that it wasn't. Once he told me congrats on rejoining the social media world, he admitted that he missed me. I was a little thrown off by the comment but bypassed it by just replying, *Thanks* with a smiley face. I guess the smiley face was the wrong move because his next questioned made my armpits sweat: *Can I take you out on a date?* I immediately refused the offer and told him that his ex-wife and I were still friends. I had already made the mistake once by having sex with someone that my best friend had sex with, so why would I do that again? After my refusal, he proceeded to claim that he and his ex-wife were divorced because she cheated on him with a Mexican while he was overseas. He drug her more into the dirt by pointing out that she had a baby by a drug dealer.

I didn't know what to say besides: *Ok, we are still friends, and I don't want this to be awkward or disrespectful.* After a few minutes of the bubbles going up and down on the messenger app, he replied: *She has moved on and she has a baby. Why can't I be happy, too?* Honestly, I didn't have a comeback for that, but I stuck to my guns. No meant no. He proceeded to tell me that I was the most beautiful and intelligent woman to him. He said that he didn't know why he was even telling me, but he felt like I should know. I screenshotted all of his messages because I wanted to send them all to his ex-wife, but I refrained. She was going through a rough pregnancy, and the last thing she needed to hear was that her ex-husband was hitting on her "associate" from work.

A week later he came back and asked again if he could take me out. I refused once more, because I just couldn't bring myself to do it. It resonated in the back of my head for a while, because he wasn't that bad looking. He was a bald Italian with a pretty smile. He was really skinny, and that's how I liked them. Moreover, he had a career and was technically single. If he would have approached me five years prior to that, I wouldn't thought twice about it, and I would let him take me out on a date. It was different this time. I had matured and was ready for "Mr. Right" not "Mr. Right Now." A few months later, he uploaded a meme to his Facebook page that read: *We'd make a beautiful interracial baby.* I had to blink several times when I saw it, because I knew he was talking about me. This was the first time someone other than the last military guy wanted more than just sex. He actually wanted to breed with me.

I sent him message: *Are you talking about me?*

He replied: *Have you thought about letting me take you on a date yet?*

At this point, the surgeon was out of the picture, and he was saying all the right things at the right time.

Me: *What do you want from me?*

As quickly as I could push send, he replied: *I want to take you out on a date. I'm ready to settle down with a woman that I deserve. You are getting your master's degree and writing blogs. I think that is so cool that you took a risk and want to do something with your life. You are beautiful, smart, and intelligent. I want to take you on a date when I come home from overseas."*

It had been a long time since someone acknowledged the hard work I put in to get where I was. Every man I came across only wanted sex from me, and I'd finally met a friend who was interested in just me. The problem was that I didn't know what I was going to do about the ex-wife. I told him I would think about it and get back to him. I called up my girls and asked their opinion. Of course, they felt the ex-wife and I weren't really friends, just associates, and if he was only asking to take me on one date, they didn't see the harm in that. I figured they were right. It was only a date, and if it didn't work out, I wouldn't sweat it nor would I have to tell her. I got back on Facebook a few days later and confirmed our first date. He was so stoked that he sent a snoopy character jumping up and down as a reply. I thought it was so corny, but it made me laugh.

From the moment I agreed to our date, we talked every single day, two times a day. He would tell me how beautiful he thought I was and how much he meditated about me in the past. He filled my soul. He made a point to make me feel important every day. We were intimate without touching each other, and that was the best part. I had never waited six months to have sex with a man, but I found that it wasn't hard. Every day I fell harder and harder for him. The emotional attachment was out of this world. Eventually, we talked about having children and getting married. I was all about my career, so marriage and kids were the last thing on my mind. Plus, Mother never got married, so I thought I would end up like her minus the two kids. I thought God had finally sent me the man of my dreams. He was funny, caring, attractive, goal-oriented, honest and open, and wanted a future with me. He catered to my every need, want and desire. I was in love, but I wasn't going to tell him that just yet.

One night while we were talking, he asked, "What if I told you that I loved you?"

My heart starting beating so fast, because I knew I felt the same way but was too scared to admit it.

Instead, I replied back to his question with a question, "What if I told you that I loved you?"

He laughed and said, "Well, I love you!"

With tears in my eyes, I replied, "I love you, too." We were officially in a relationship six days before my birthday. He bought me some flowers, and although the iPad came early, that was a part of my birthday gift as well. Everything seemed to flow and while on the outside it looked as if things were moving fast, I felt everything was right. We continued to talk about getting married the following year, although I wanted to get married after I was finished with school, he insisted. We picked out baby names and started writing out our wedding lists. I had even put a deposit of a thousand dollars down on our reception hall. I was very tight with my money, but I felt in my heart that I truly loved someone who loved me, so it was no big deal. Love didn't have a price tag. I started to pick out wedding dresses and showed him what I thought I'd look beautiful in on our wedding day. He agreed that I would be a gorgeous bride. I had a partner, and I couldn't believe that in a year I was going to marry the man of my dreams.

He hadn't proposed, because he was overseas, but Christmas day couldn't come fast enough. Although he probably wasn't supposed to tell me, his plan was to propose on Christmas. He even told his mother that I looked like Christmas morning. When I worked with his ex-wife, she said his family didn't like her because she was black. I wasn't concerned, because I knew if they didn't like me, it was going to be their problem not mine. I was in love with him, and he was in love with me.

I thought to myself that even though my father wasn't around, he would at least know his responsibility of me was almost no longer his. I was about to be the responsibility of another man. A man with character, a man with integrity, a man who saw my beautiful soul, a man who catches my tears in my weakest moments and praises me for all my achievements. I was already whole, but I felt fulfilled. I had encountered many men but none that fulfilled me. We were so in love that I even told Mother how I felt about him. Mother and I never talked about the men in my life. She never asked, and I never told. I felt majority of the men who came along weren't worthy enough to meet Mother. To be honest, sometimes I was just embarrassed.

Every day that it got closer for him to come home, my anxiety grew. Not in a bad way either. I was just anticipating physically seeing him after ten years. He was the man who loved me and cherished me. The man who saved me from a cold world of heartless men, even my father. It was a new day, I was a new woman, and I was ready to move on with my new man. We didn't talk to the ex-wife, but I was leaving that up to him at that point. He was going to hear her backlash when he picked up the dogs from her upon his return. They still maintained a friendship and shared dogs, so I was fine with their ability to still communicate after her cheating scandal. I thought that was so big of him, although he made it clear that cheating was grounds to end the relationship; therefore, I made sure I was strapped down. Tight. It also helped that I still stayed with my supervisor from the nursing home. It was the "No boys allowed" zone.

I was starting to see the changes in my behaviors. I worked harder in school, and I didn't only think about me,

I thought about us. I went and got an apartment, because I knew he was coming home and bringing him to my supervisor's house was a no-go, and I knew I had to make it work. I could have just spend the night with his family every night when he came home, but I wanted to us to have "adult time" by ourselves. I wanted to show him that I was the woman he could trust and the most important woman in his life besides his mother. He had mentioned before that it was important to him that his mother and the woman he loved got along, because she hated everyone that he dated. I was going to be different. I was the one. Not because that's what I thought, but because that's what he thought. He bragged about me to his fellow unit and even sent his mother a message to let her know there was a new sheriff in town, and I was there to stay. Forever.

When he called my phone, it was the first time I heard his voice on the other end. He was so excited to be back in the states, and I was excited for him to be back. I was catching my flight in a few days to go visit him before he came back home for two months to visit his family. When he called, I was thrilled. We always called each other babe. It was our little thing. He had rented a car and booked a hotel, so we didn't have to stay on base. I was leaving in three days, and I was vowing to myself to not have sex with him until we at least went on the date. We waited six months anyway, so what was a few more hours?

I needed to make a grand entrance, and I had the perfect idea. I wanted him to know that I loved him for being patient and loving me. I wanted the world to know he was all mine. I went to Walmart and purchased the brightest shirt I could. I printed out a shirt with a picture of him on it making a funny face. I purchased letters that I glued on the shirt. It read: *My hero* under his picture. It was the best I could do the night before my flight to my destination. I only got a few hours asleep, because it took all night for me to make the shirt. My supervisor drove me to the airport, and I told her that I'd let her know when I landed safely. Each way had two stops, and each time I stopped at an airport, people kept staring at my shirt. I wasn't sure if it because it was a white man with a funny face or because it was a bright shirt. The flight attendant even asked me if he knew I was wearing the shirt. I told her it was a surprise.

I got off the plane and my heart was beating fast from nervousness. I wasn't the skinny 120lb girl he met ten years ago. Yes, we used FaceTime, but it was nothing like seeing someone in real life. Touching them for the first time. Holding them for the first time. Kissing them the first time, especially someone that you loved. I was walking through the airport looking for a man in army attire. My eyelash was falling off, so I was hoping he didn't notice when I walked up. Then, I spotted him. He was blushing red and smiling from ear to ear. I was so shy seeing him the first time, that I couldn't even look, but he made me by leaning forward to kiss me. He grabbed my hand, and we walked over to get my luggage. We held each other like we couldn't really believe it was happening. At least I couldn't. While waiting by baggage claim, I texted my supervisor and told her I was safe. Safe with the only man who ever cared about me.

We got my luggage and headed off to the hotel. He didn't notice my shirt until we got there, and I was too nervous to point out to him when we first saw each other.

"No girl has ever done this for me. Hold on. Let me take a picture of it."

He was so stunned by my creativity and thoughtfulness.

"Oh yeah, I wanted to surprise you and show you that I'm all yours babe."

He grinned from ear to ear again and said he was sending the picture to his mother. It took a while to get our hotel, but finally we got our key and was headed to the fourth floor which was a VIP access. When we got into our room, it was more like a mini apartment. We had a small kitchen with a cherry wood table. We had a living room with drapes covering the window and a bathroom with a Jacuzzi tub and shower with four shower heads. We also had a king size canopy bed with a luxurious bed set decorated with eight pillows. Our room even had a built in fireplace and a closet with mirrors as its doors. I had stayed in nice hotels but nothing like this. As I kept looking around, it was clear to me that I was where I wanted to be.

He grabbed me from behind and whispered, "I'm just trying to show you that I want to marry you."

I turned around, looked him in the eyes, and smiled. He kissed me like he loved me. It felt so different. So real. I knew my whole vow to "wait until after dinner" had gone out the door. His hands went under my shirt, and I started to quiver. It had been six months, and I could feel my orgasm coming before he took off my pants. I hopped onto the bed, and he got on top of me. He took off my shirt and pulled down my leggings. He removed his shirt, boots, and army pants. I never looked down to see how big it was, since he said the last woman he was in love with used him for sex, so I knew he wouldn't disappoint. He sucked on my breasts, and I could hardly breathe. His fingers caressed my body and I knew I couldn't make him stop. I didn't want him to stop. He slid down between my legs and opened them, but I wasn't ready for him to lick me just yet since I hadn't showered after flying all day. He didn't seem bothered by my denial of oral sex.

He put his fingers in, and my eyes widened not only from the sensation that shot through my body, but from the fact that nothing had entered that particular hole in six months. The man I was going to marry was getting ready to enter me for the first time. I wasn't scared to look him in the eyes. I felt vulnerable for the first time in a long time. He put spit on his hand and although I should have stopped him because spit normally gave women bacterial infections, I didn't. I didn't want to disturb the perfect moment. He rubbed that hand on his genital area and entered into me so deeply that he touched my heart. From that moment on, my life took a dramatic turn. When Christmas Day came, I couldn't wait to be the woman he would soon call his Mrs.

I woke up the day next feeling like a new woman. We had our first physically intimate moment, and I knew this was the man I would be with for the rest of my life. God did well this time. He had a stable a career, he catered to my needs physically, emotionally, and financially, and we had instant chemistry once we created our soul tie. Although we were in a long distance relationship until I finished my master's program, it seemed to be working in our favor. I couldn't wait until he came back home to spend quality time with my family and I. I didn't know how his mother was going to take me, but I was going to put on the "white girl" act and let her know her son was all mine.

"Hurry up and get dressed woman," he demanded.

I quickly ran into the bathroom with my soap and razor. I couldn't wait to get all dolled up for my boo. I turned on the water and let all four sprayers hit my body. As I lathered the soap onto my hand and rubbed it between my legs, there was a slight difference. The lips of my vagina seemed puffy. I had sensed irritation the night before after our first encounter, but I just assumed it was a bit of irritation from his spit. As I quickly rubbed my hand all over my body and under my armpits, I rinsed off and hopped out the shower to get dressed. I was going to make the best of our stay while he was in the states.

We went to dinner, rented movies, and practiced yoga because he was a huge fan of releasing stress and toxins from the body. He took me to get a facial and massage, and we had more sex. It such a fantastic four days, but there was one small issue. My irritation had become a burning sensation when I urinated, and my lips had gotten even bigger. It was to the point that I would hold off on going to the bathroom as long as I could, because it was so painful. I had never had anything like this happen to me before. I was not sure what type of bacterial infection had occurred, but this one was brutal. I knew for sure I hadn't been intimate with anyone since the surgeon, and he had been on overseas, so there was no way he could have been intimate with anyone. I was sure this would disappear by the time I flew back home, and if not, I would just go to the doctor to take those nasty horse pills to get rid of the infection. Yes, that's the plan, I thought as I kissed him goodbye.

We stared into each other's eyes as I walked up the escalator to go through airport security. I was already missing him, and we hadn't even been away from each other for more than two seconds. He mouthed, "I love you," and I said the same in return. I was going back home to let my family know my trip was awesome and that I was by far the happiest I had been with a man in very long time. Phones calls, texts, and pow-wows were on the top of the list to tell everyone how great my stay was with my boyfriend. I was thrilled to let everyone the search had ended and that the glow they had noticed on my face for the past six months was real. Everyone seemed so happy for me and thought I had deserved all the happiness in the world. I couldn't help but to think that all the heartache I went through without my father being present, the struggles of surviving while being raised by Mother and being lusted after by any man who paid me attention, was all worth it for this moment.

I was on cloud nine, but there was still a little problem that I couldn't seem to solve. My genital area was on fire, and I could find any amount of water to put it out. I called my best friend's sister, the one that looked like Pocahontas. She was a nurse.

She and I discussed my symptoms, and then she said with an offensive tone, "Bitch, did he give you something?"

I quickly denied the accusation. I knew he was overseas and wasn't with anyone, and I knew for sure that my hoeing days were over, so we just came to the conclusion that it was just an infection which was an easy fix.

That night things became more than just a quick fix. I woke up in a puddle of urine the next morning. I was so confused. I knew that I'd had a bacterial infection before, but it had never went this far. Something was wrong, and I couldn't hold off any longer. I was headed to the doctor. I had gotten a checkup earlier that year in March, so I knew there were no possibilities of an STD. I was a little nervous with having a male doctor examine my private area, but it had to be done. Luckily, he was a nice guy and used humor to make me comfortable. It worked. As he and his assistant examined me, he asked me a few questions.

"When did the symptoms start?"

I replied, "A week ago."

He then asked was I intimate, and I confirmed that I was. I told him I was in a relationship and had not been sexually active in six months and the symptoms started after the first time my boyfriend and I had sex. I confessed that he had come back from overseas. The doctor asked if my boyfriend was "checked" before being released back into the states. As far as I knew, he got checked since it was mandatory procedure. The doctor then told me he would test me for everything to rule out a few things, but he did confirm I had a bladder infection which caused me to involuntarily urinate on myself. I had never had one of those before, and I damn sure didn't want one again. That was the worst feeling in the world, and I wouldn't wish it on my worst enemy. The doctor told me to call back in a week for results. I collected my doctor excuse and went to work.

My boyfriend wouldn't be home until the week of Thanksgiving, so I knew the next two weeks would drag, but I was wrong. He got a call from his mother stating that his grandmother had died. Therefore, he had to put a rush on his orders so he could get home. Although it was sad news, I was secretly happy. It meant we were going to spend more time together before he went to his next base to start his masters and complete his captain's course. This would be the first holiday I would spend with him, and I couldn't wait to show everyone the man who put the glow on my face. A week passed and it was time for him to fly home, because his grandmother's funeral was the next day. I also needed to get my results from the doctor to ensure I only had a bacterial infection. I went on my lunch break and made the phone call. I was really confident since the burning and pain had stopped after they injected some medication into my left butt cheek.

The office receptionist answered the phone and asked for my name. I identified myself and told her that I was calling to get results from last week's checkup. She put me on hold for a few minutes, and then came back with my results. The words that came out of her mouth changed my life forever. I blinked my eyes in shock. Actually, I went deaf and couldn't understand anything else after that moment. I asked if I could call her back but hung up before she could even reply. I didn't know what to say or who to tell. Everything I ever worked for and the perfect relationship I thought I had was a waste. My past had finally caught up to me, and karma had come back and bit me right in the ass, literally. I was that girl. I was the girl who caught an STD that she couldn't get rid of. I only knew one other person who had it, so I called them to cry my heart out. She told me it would be okay and that I would get through it, but that wasn't what I wanted to hear. The only good news I had was that it wasn't HIV or AIDS (thank God). I would have jumped off a bridge.

After I hung up with my friend who I now shared a common ailment with, I called back to the doctors' office. I told her I was ready to hear any helpful information she had to help me get through the worst day of my life. She explained that I was type II and that there was no way I could confirm who I might have gotten the STD from based on the nature of the virus. She explained that it was possible that I'd had the STD for a long time and didn't know since I never had a breakout before now. The nurse stated that most people do not know that they have this STD until an outbreak happens, which is what my friend told me on the phone while I was crying. The nurse also told me an outbreak happens when your immune system is low or when you are stressed. I started to think back to the last time I was sick and drew a blank. I did, however, have a tooth pulled a few weeks before flying to Texas to see my boyfriend and was taking medication to help the pain. Maybe that was it. Maybe that was why I had an outbreak. Before I hung up, she also stated that my boyfriend could have been the carrier without knowing due to men not having many breakouts. I was convinced it was me who was diseased, and I had to tell the love of my life that I had just ruined his life.

I got into my car and texted him: *Please call me. It's important.* I swallowed hard and tried to clear my throat and wipe my tears before telling him the hard truth.

"Babe, what is it?" he said when I answered the phone.

As I began to break down all over again, I blurted out through spit, slobber, and tears that I had called the doctor and received my results which came back as positive for a life-long STD. I made sure to tell him that it wasn't AIDS or HIV, but I felt like it was and at any minute I was going to die. I already felt like I had died inside. I had the perfect guy, the perfect career, and the perfect life, and it all ended with one phone call.

I took a deep breath and forcibly yelled, "TELL ME RIGHT NOW IF THIS IS GOING TO BE OVER! THERE IS NO NEED TO DRAG THIS OUT, I NEED TO KNOW IF THIS IS OVER!

He held the phone in silence, then he calmly told me he was getting ready to board the plane and wanted to think about it on the way home. As I continued to cry, I said okay and hung up the phone. I tried to pull my thoughts together and go back to work. It didn't work. I was empty inside all day. I was going to have to face my family and tell them my perfect relationship was ending, because I hurt the person I grew to love the most. I failed everyone, even my father who was absent. His princess was no longer a princess. She was tampered, dirty, and diseased.

I arrived at the airport at midnight with my eyes full of tears. I was unaware that this would be my first encounter with his parents. When he came through the airport, I felt like the word "failure" was written on my forehead. He grabbed my hand and walked me over to his parents and sister and introduced us. I put on a fake smile, because I knew if I started crying, they would have been confused. He stood there holding me, because he could see the sadness in my eyes. I didn't want to have the talk, but I knew once he spotted his luggage on the rotating belt in baggage claim, it was do or die. I didn't want to die, although the news gave me a new death reaction, so I had no other choice but to pull my big girl panties up and face the truth. His parents drove his truck and he got into my car. We didn't even get out the parking lot before the conversation started, and I busted out into tears. He remained calm as I let out my frustration, disappointment, and sadness. I pled my case that I hadn't been with anyone the entire time we were together, and still he remained calm. He didn't ask any questions, nor did his emotion change. This was odd but I was so disoriented, I didn't even notice.

His only response was, "I have been with over thirty women. Maybe this is a sign that I need to settle down. I don't want to break up. I want to work through this. This is ours together."

Although I was still distraught, I let out a sigh of relief. He didn't become angry. He didn't think I was a filthy hoe. He didn't even question if we would spend our lives together. He just went into the supportive role as my soon to be husband, and I couldn't have asked God for a better half. Unfortunately, his parents lived on a lake, and we had to travel on the hilly roads. They were slick and icy, and I hadn't purchased new tires yet. We had to have his parents pull over at the Speedway gas station, so we could hop in the truck and travel the rest of the way to his parents' home. Since, I was able to breathe after that conversation, I got into the truck able to make a little conversation with his parents and sister. Since I cried for twelve hours straight, I was ready to cuddle with the man I loved. The man who had my back. The man who was better half.

We went to his grandmother's funeral the next day and I was able to smile as I was introduced to his entire family on his mother's side. I felt like we were at our wedding already, because he was dressed in his uniform. It reminded me of the prince in *Cinderella,* and I was standing beside him being his supportive "play wife." Everyone came up to us and shook our hands as if we had just gotten married. They all kept asking if I was his fiancée. We both said no and laughed, because we knew we wanted to get married but not right at that moment. We went to the hotel after the funeral was over. We'd had a long day, so it was time to relax. However, before we rested, he wanted to conduct an inspection. I had been taking these white horse pills with some applesauce for four days. I was never good at swallowing pills with water, so I had to crush them up in food.

He motioned me to come into the sitting area of our hotel room.

"Let me see it."

I was confused by his demand.

"Let you see what?"

He looked at me square in the face and said, "You know what I want to see, so lay down on the floor and open your legs."

The swelling had gone down and most of the red spots had disappeared. I laid down on the floor and timidly opened my legs. Even though he had already been inside me, I would have been beet red from the embarrassment if I were white. He didn't care. He took down his pants and stuck it inside. I was a little dumbfounded by his actions. If the roles were reversed, I don't think I would have been able to do it, especially if someone was having an outbreak. Once he came inside me, we got up and went to bed. It was officially our disease.

Chapter 13 – Diamonds are Forever

It was vacation time, and we were set to go to California for four days. He initially asked me to go on this trip when we first started chatting, but I wasn't sure about it at the time. Since we'd made things official, I was packed and ready to go. We didn't make any reservations at any hotels. We were just going to make the trip up as we went. The main thing we had to make sure was that we were traveling Highway 1 while we were sight-seeing. The only problem was that I didn't know Highway 1 was on mountains. I was deathly afraid of heights, and he seemed to have left that small detail out when he was explaining what we would be doing.

As we came upon our first beach it was a magical sight to see. It was scene that I had never before seen, and it was breathtaking. We saw another couple on the beach and another male who was completely naked. Apparently it was a norm in California, because he walked past us like he was fully dressed. We put our feet in the water and took many pictures to create memories.

As he kissed me on my forehead, he softly said, "We should get married here."

Although that sounded like a good idea, I still wanted a traditional wedding where I walked down the aisle. Plus, how the hell is my family supposed to afford flying to California? I knew that wasn't going to be a good idea.

We went on to the next beach and continued to travel Highway 1 for two days. I had several panic attacks and had to sit in the backseat at some point, because I was too afraid to look out the window. He was so mad at me, but I knew I would just freak out if I sat in the front seat. We would get to different stopping points, and if it wasn't too scary, I would join him in snapping pictures of the beautiful scene. Then, I would quickly run back to the car as if I was being chased. We stopped at a small town called Monterey. We thought it would be a cool baby name. They had an aquarium which was very interesting and informative. We got to see all types of fish and sharks, and we even saw seals get fed. We hadn't been having sex, so that was the first night we had sex in a few weeks. He didn't seem interested, but I was horny, so I pushed his resistance to the side and got what I wanted.

The next day, we kept traveling and sight-seeing. We got to the last beach called Pismo Beach and our hotel had an ocean view. It was the best view in the world. We walked the beach holding hands, and ate dinner at a restaurant that had a menu that looked like it was written in a different language. We face-timed his parents and since I had already spent Thanksgiving at their home, I was able to open up and hold a conversation with them. I was so appreciative of him taking me on the trip, that I wrote a note and stuck it in his small bag that he used for his toiletries. I loved him, and I needed him to know I was all in.

After our four day trip to California, we finished our weekend with a trip to Las Vegas to celebrate Mr. Cooper's birthday. He was turning twenty-five and wanted to go out with a bang. So, we hopped on the plane and headed to the city that never sleeps. I had never been to Vegas, but one thing I did know was there were no mountains. There was just alcohol and a whole lot of gambling and partying, and I was down for that. When we arrived, Mr. Cooper and all of his friends were already out drinking. We decided to go out and explore the city on our own before we met up to head to the club. The streets were packed with people and various impersonators. Our hotel was attached to a mall, so we really didn't have to step outside if we didn't want to. Of course Las Vegas is known for gambling, but I wasn't interested in that. I just wanted to soak it all in and have a good time with my friends and my man.

After a few hours of walking around, we went back to the hotel to get dressed. I put on a red dress that fit tight to every curve I had. I wanted to be the black version of Jessica Rabbit, and I was ready to make an appearance. We had VIP access to the club, because Mr. Cooper and I knew the DJ who grew up in our home town. He set us up with a VIP table and our drinks were free all night. I was having so much fun that I started dancing on top of the tables. The club was packed with people of all cultures. I was in heaven and could do this all week. As we kept dancing, a group of black females walked in and sat next to our VIP table. They were celebrating a birthday and seemed to be having fun. They eventually became friendly with our table and the night took off. Unfortunately, I felt that my man was becoming too friendly. He kept trying to hook Mr. Cooper up with one of the girls, and I was starting to wonder why he was so concerned with hooking them up.

He could sense my irritation, so he said, "Babe, I'm just trying to hook your boy up for his birthday. Don't worry. I love you. I'm here with you!"

Although, I knew he liked black women, I never thought he would be so concerned with hooking up my male best friend with a black woman when he knows his interest is more with white women. That night I was not too thrilled with him, but he made it up by climbing on top of me for three minutes of sex. It wasn't the best, but I was in Vegas. What happens in Vegas, stays in Vegas.

The next night we went to the club, but I wasn't as interested because I was so tired. We had a long week and our flight was the next morning. We left the bar early, and when we got back to the hotel, I was knocked into a coma. I didn't hear or see anything once my head hit the pillow until 8 a.m. then next day. We heard a knock at the door. At first I thought it was housekeeping, but when he opened the door, Mr. Cooper and his friends came hopping into our room with drinks in their hands, spinning around in circles. I barely had my eyes open, but I was so confused as to why they were still awake and in the clothes they wore to the bar the night before. Come to find out they went to an after-hours bar that stayed open until

6 a.m. They continued to party while our old asses went back to the hotel. I was salty that I couldn't stay awake long enough. My feet were hurting, and it was getting cold. I couldn't hang and that morning definitely showed it. We packed our things and said our goodbyes as we headed back home to where things were about to get real.

I had school the next weekend, and he wanted to come up and stay the night with me. He always had a bad feeling while he was overseas that I was seeing someone when I stayed in a hotel while I went to school. I figured he had trust issues since he told me his first wife cheated on him, so letting him come along was no issue for me, because I knew I was faithful. This was the first time in my life that I was dedicating my whole self to someone. At times, I didn't recognize who I was, because I fell so hard. However, I couldn't deny the new woman I was becoming. After we went to dinner that night and I went to school the next day, everything seemed to be going perfect. Christmas day was around the corner, and I had all of his presents he wanted, wrapped and ready to go.

I was still at the nursing home, so I had to work Christmas day. The night before, I decided I would stay the night with him and spend Christmas morning with him and his family. We ate dinner and went to church. I was started to feel like I was becoming a part of the family, and I felt that I belonged. I felt wanted and loved, and there was no better feeling than that. When we got back to his parent's house, I slipped into my Hello Kitty onesie. I laid down with him on the futon that his parents had for him downstairs in their basement when he came home from overseas. We laid there for a while and he began to kiss me softly. I could feel him getting hard, and I knew what was getting ready to happen. Everything was usually routine, but this time something was different.

He looked me in the eyes and said, "You know that I love you right?"

Very slowly, I replied, "Yes."

For the next half hour, he made love to me like he had never done before. I know he had talked about proposing on Christmas, so I wasn't sure if he was just preparing for my surprise moment the next day. One thing I did know was that he loved me and I loved him.

The next morning, I brought his gifts inside so we could all open our gifts together. I bought him a blanket, gift card, sound machine, and a digital camera, and said a poem while he opened his gifts. His parents were so thrilled, and they were almost in tears. He stood up and said no one had ever done anything like that for him, and I smiled big, feeling accomplished. He got me a lot of gifts, and although they were lovely gifts, the one and only gift I thought I was getting, I didn't get. I didn't ask because even though I wanted to get married to him, I had the jitters about him proposing, especially in front of his parents. I was kind of relieved because the feeling of not being ready came into mind, and I'm pretty sure that's not the feeling I was supposed to have about the man I love. He gave me all my gifts and one of them was in a small box. My heart started beating super-fast, and I just knew I wasn't going to be able to open this small box without feeling overwhelmed. Luckily, the little box was only perfume. I felt the timing was right, and if he was to propose I wanted it to be a surprise.

After our great morning on Christmas, we met up with my friends back in my hometown. We drank beers and listened to music all night. Everything was going well until he pulled me to the side and started to talk about our future decisions. We had this conversation before but his tone was different this time.

"Keshia, I am really serious about having a family. I really want a family. I don't know if you know how serious I am, but I'm very serious about this."

I knew we had talked about having a baby, but I figured it wouldn't be until after I graduated from school and when we said, "I do." I calmly agreed that I wanted a family too and assured him we would have one eventually.

He then told me that he gave another girl a ring before, and she left with the ring. I was confused because I had only known him to be in one serious relationship, and that was with his ex-wife. I was shocked by his honesty but maintained a poker face. I didn't want him to know that his confession about proposing to another woman stabbed me in the gut.

After Christmas, we continued to spend every day with each other. Our time was dwindling, because he was going to another base to finish his Captain's course and start his master's program. We went to my class reunion and brought in the New Year with a bang. Somehow that night, the proposal was addressed again. This time, he hit me in the face with a knockout punch that caused me to struggle to hold my tears back.

In a nasty tone, he said. "Keshia, you are not getting a ring before I leave to go to my next base. We need to focus more on our relationship and not just one day."

I knew Christmas was not the right time to propose, but I still wanted to eventually marry him. I was sort of baffled by his certainty of our future plans needing to be put on hold, when six days prior, he had just cried about wanting to have a family. I didn't know where our relationship was going, and after that night, I'd had enough of his uncertainty and doubts. I mean after all, I wasn't the one who begged to be in the relationship, nor asked to get married and have a family. So, one day after having another shitty conversation about marriage, he finally came out and told me that marriage did not equal commitment, only a baby did. I was speechless. I had goals and dreams, and he basically gave me an ultimatum. It's either a baby or no relationship.

The next morning I woke up at 6 a.m. I couldn't sleep because I had a lot of thoughts running through my mind. I didn't know if I should be thrilled that he wanted me to bear his children or to be running out the door getting far away. All I did know was that having a baby didn't guarantee commitment, and Mother was a prime example of that. I also know he would have to be away for long periods of time, so my children would grow up without a father just like I did. After I calmed down and we went to church, we had a reasonable conversation about the next step. I let him know that I did love him and reminded him that all the marriage talk was his idea from the beginning. After he snapped back into his senses, we agreed that I could go dress shopping, because September was only nine months away and my girlfriends had to start looking for bridesmaids' dresses.

After he left, I was excited to go dress shopping with my best friends. I didn't tell anyone about the blow up we had, because I was determined to show him that I was wife material and not just good enough to only birth his children. I had worked my ass off to prove that point and sacrificed a lot. I even quit the nursing home job I'd had for the past nine years, so I could visit him each month while he was completing his Captain's course. Too many of my friends and family were invested in my first "real" relationship, and I just wasn't going to let it slip through the cracks. He had everything I wanted in a man, unlike the other goofballs I wasted my time with. Needless to say, I went dress shopping and found my dress. It didn't take me long, because I knew what I wanted. I had never imagined myself getting married but this was my chance.

I wanted a fairytale wedding with a Cinderella theme, because I felt I had found my prince. I knew exactly what I wanted him to wear and what colors I wanted our wedding to be decorated with. We had already had our venue book which was magical with its tall white pillars, so everything was all falling into place. All I needed was a proposal, and I was sure that it was coming, since he agreed for me to purchase a dress. I let him know that I had purchased a dress, and he begged to see it. Of course it's bad luck to let the man see the dress, so I refused. However, I was willing to show him my other ideas, so he booked a flight for me to go see him the first weekend in

February. I had school during Valentine's Day weekend, so this was the only time we could visit with each other before my next visit in March.

I flew there on a Friday, and we had sushi for dinner that night. I shared the things I wanted us to have at the wedding and began to get excited that he was on board with what I had picked. The next morning, I had a surprise for him, since I wasn't able to spend Valentine's Day with him because of school. I made him a scrapbook of our vacation in California and Vegas, and hid the money he paid for my plane ticket all around his house. The goal of the game was to tell him where the money was hidden, but only if he showed me that he had bought a ring. Unfortunately, that didn't work out in my favor, and again I was heartbroken. It wasn't until he saw the hurt in my eyes that pulled himself together. He told me that if he loves me, he should show me, so he drove us to the mall. We went inside, and once again, I was trying on rings. I had to go to the bathroom, and the saleswoman pointed in its direction. I couldn't find it and eventually had to ask an employee for assistance. By the time I returned, he had bought the ring.

He got down on one knee in the mall and said, "Keshia, will you marry me?"

I said yes with my eyes full of tears. He finally did it, and I couldn't believe it was real. I was now an engaged woman. He called his parents, and I called all my friends. I even put it on Facebook even though social media was not my go to when I had a 'boo," but this one was different. I had a man who was willing to protect me in my weakest moments and celebrate all my successes. I finally had a man who stepped up in my life to be the man I always wanted my father to be.

The Guide
To Getting over an Absentee Father

Yes, I know. You're probably wondering why I didn't go into further detail about the man who was supposed to carry my heart forever and the details of my fairytale wedding. I figured I'd save that story for my next book that will be released in 2016. I just wanted to make sure you know that you can find true love when you start loving yourself and apply all the tips in this guide to elevate your womanhood. After making countless mistakes and having anger and bitterness toward your father for being absent and your mother for struggling to take care of you, you have to finally say enough is enough. Something has to change. You can't step forward and continue to be reminded of your past. So, here are some ways that helped me break the cycle. I believe full-heartedly that you can benefit from applying these tips to your life. As you read each tip, write down ways to incorporate it into your life.

1. Surround yourself with positive people.

It is so important to surround yourself with people who have your best interest at heart. These are the people who are going to make sure you are making the right decisions while modeling positive behaviors themselves. My father was in and out of jail, and my mother was so busy worrying about our survival, so I couldn't ask them to be in my corner. Luckily for me, the track families, particularly the dentist and his family, were my saving grace. They kept me on my Ps and Qs and made sure I stayed on the right path to attend college, and they held me accountable for completing college. They were my motivation, and when things got tough financially and emotionally, they stayed in my corner.

I know what you're thinking though. You're just not ready to get rid the particular group of friends that you have such a "good time" with on a regular basis. Well, for now, I won't ask you to get rid of them, but I will challenge you by asking how are your friends helping you achieve your goals? Are they doing more deposits or withdrawals (emotionally and spiritually)? When was the last time you called them for some mature, reasonable advice that was helpful to your growth? If you can't think of any, then you need to reevaluate the people you surround yourself with. See, these are the friends who haven't quite figured life out yet, and they frequently find themselves in drama or in trouble. Hanging with a toxic group friends who hasn't quite grabbed life by the horns is stunting your growth. Surround yourself with those friends or people who make you want to be a better person in all areas of your life. Particularly share your time with the ones who motivate you to achieve your dreams. These are the people you want in your corner, so when life throws you lemons, you have a team to help you make lemonade.

2. Take as many positive risks as you can.

When I say I used to live in a box, I really did. I was scared to do anything I wasn't familiar with doing. I just wasn't a risk taker, because my parents never were. What I did for eighteen years was model their behavior. I didn't see anything wrong with my close-mindedness, until I was asked to do something that made me feel uncomfortable. By then, I was in my early 20s, and I had to move away to finish school. I had a difficult decision to make, either I was going to throw my hands up in the air and yell, "NOPE! I'M NOT MOVING AWAY FROM MY FAMILY AND FRIENDS!" or I was going to suck it up and move to a new town with new people and become the first college graduate of my family.

I chose option two, and I am glad I did. If I hadn't taken that route, I wouldn't have written this book, nor would I have applied to graduate school. I could have missed out on so many opportunities and the blessings God had for me. So, I encourage you to take as many positive risks as possible, because you don't know what God has for you. You don't want to miss out on learning something new, and believe me, there is a lot to learn in this world. During my risk-taking, I learned how to book my first flight at age 28. I had flown a few times before, which I was deathly afraid of doing, but I had always made the person I was flying with or going to see book my ticket. Therefore, I never had to learn how to book a flight on my own. I know it sounds small, but traveling - especially traveling by airplane - is something my family just didn't do. Today, I can proudly say that I can book my own airline ticket and fly wherever I want without hesitation. Take risks whether big or small, because you never know what God has for you once you gain the knowledge obtained from being a risk-taker.

3. Set standards when dating.

Since my father was absent and I had to watch my mother raise my sister and I by herself, I wasn't exactly prepped on how to set standards for dating. I had what you called "situationships." I say situationships, because technically none of them were real relationships. The common thing that I found while in these "situationships," was that I didn't set standards while dating, because I was never taught to do so. I just accepted anything and anyone who paid me any attention, but I'll be the first to tell you that all attention is not good attention. I was looking for love in all the wrong places and ended up going through heartbreaks repeatedly. It got to the point that my emotional walls were so strong, that even a wrecking ball couldn't tear them down. It didn't matter if a dude sold drugs, abused drugs, or was with other women while he was with me. Hell, the dude didn't even have to take me out on a date majority of the time. I just didn't care. Fortunately, as I started to grow professionally, I realized that these weren't the type of men that I wanted to take to a work function or bring around my family - especially the dentist and his family. I started to recognize that I was a hard worker, and I was sure to make the right decisions to position myself to have a better life, so why wasn't I demanding the same for the guy I was dating? I know, it makes no sense, right?

To help you refrain from making the same mistakes I have or if you already did, it's important for you to understand that when you're dating, you have to set standards. If you accept anything, trust me you will get anything. When a person knows they can walk all over you and treat you any type of way, they will. I know from experience. If he is only calling you after 10:00pm (booty call hours), after you have already asked once to stop it, throw him in the discard pile and keep moving without feeling bad about it. If he can't simply plan a date, toss him in the discard pile, too. You need a leader, a provider, and a protector. If he isn't in the position to provide all three, then he is not in the position to be in your life. Period.

4. *Love yourself unconditionally*

I get it that your father is supposed to be your first love, but when you grow up without one, the chances of you loving yourself becomes slim to none when you start searching for love everywhere else but within yourself. As a woman, loving yourself is the single-handedly most important thing you could ever do. Being comfortable with who you are and your position in life is the first start. I know it may be tough when you see men only running after women with over 100k followers on Instagram, or the women who show their "assets" all over the internet and get thousands of smiley faces with the hearts as eyes underneath, but you can't compare yourself to them. Just compare yourself to the woman you see in the mirror every day and vow to make her better every chance you get. If you have freckles, love them. If you have dark skin, love it. If you have long hair or short hair, love that too. If you only have one leg, love the one leg you do have. If you have a gap in your teeth or a mole above your upper lip, love it. Whatever flaws you have, love them all and most importantly love yourself.

5. Set Goals

Two years ago, I took a black permanent marker and wrote down four to five goals I wanted to achieve within a year. These goals consisted of getting a new car, renting a house (I wasn't ready to purchase, however, renting a house was at least a glimpse of what it's like to have a home of my own), writing a book, and getting into graduate school. I was able to accomplish these goals, because I was able to hold myself accountable. Let me repeat that again. I was able to hold MYSELF accountable. I figured no one would just hand me the goals I wanted, so I had to go out there and get it myself. Setting goals and achieving them also gives you an ego booster. It helps you realize you can do it! You can break the cycle! If you want something, set a goal, and then put a plan together on how you are going to achieve it. And there's no rush either. Slow progress is better than no progress. Just keep moving toward that goal, and you will be not only satisfied with yourself, but you will get what you want out of life and hopefully be an example to others.

6. Gain control of your life and find peace and freedom.

I had to stop blaming my father for his absence and my mother for her poor choices. I realized that by doing that, it kept me stagnant, and I continued to provide excuses for my poor choices when I should have known right from wrong. I also had to get to a place where I was happy with myself and wouldn't stop until I got there. When you do what makes you happy, I swear life becomes easier and other people become irrelevant. Be responsible for your actions and evaluate how you felt when your father wasn't there for you. Be sure not to set your children up for the same circumstances. You will feel better knowing that you took a different approach to lead a different life.

7. Recognize destructive thoughts and behaviors that keep you stuck and unhappy.

I didn't think I was attractive at all, because I was dark-skinned, had short nappy hair, and big lips. Chile, let me tell you! A chick can't tell me nothing now, because women of all races would kill for my features! Although people complimented me all the time, I didn't believe it until I started to tell myself that I was beautiful and was worth having a good guy in my life. Plus, I had worked my ass off to achieve all my goals, so why would I think I was worth nothing? That's the question you need to ask yourself. Why don't you think you deserve better? Why are you putting yourself in situations or surrounding yourself with people who are negative and not making you happy? Change your thoughts. You are beautiful. Change your surroundings and push past people who are stuck. You are valuable and worth it, and when you believe this, you will become free and happy.

8. Believe in yourself and find your purpose.

You can do it! Don't give up! Life is never easy, and no one will give you anything. You must be able to work for everything you want. Trust me, I know. I had to keep telling myself this over and over again to get through undergraduate school. No one I knew had gone as far as I did with my life, so I had no choice but to believe I could make it through, even if no one else thought I could. When trying to find your purpose, I honestly believe people get passion and purpose mixed up. Passion is what you aspire to do and purpose is what you're called to do by God. I always had a passion to work with families and be a social worker. However, I believe my purpose is that God placed it on my heart to write a book revealing my story to help others who have grown up in a similar environment as myself. Writing this book was a feeling that I couldn't shake. If I chose to keep denying this feeling, I would be denying God's purpose for me. I encourage you to get in tune with God and find your purpose, because you have one.

9. *You are not alone.*

Growing up without my father, my mother not tending to my emotional nor financial needs, and being in and out of broken relationships, became a very cold and lonely world. When you become disappointed with your life, you think you're all alone and that no one can relate to you, but I'm here to tell you that's not true. You will never be alone because number one, God is always with you, and He hears your prayers, thoughts, and cries. Secondly, there are others who have been in your same predicament. You are never alone, and if no one wants to stand with you, remember God is always with you.

10. *Coping with the feelings of anger toward your father.*

It's okay to be angry that your father was not around. I was angry a lot. Just make sure you don't remain so angry that you became stagnant in life. Also, try not to remain in worthless relationships because you are expecting the no-good man to fulfill the void. It is important to also evaluate how your father was raised. If he grew up without a father, it will go one of two ways. He will be a great father or a deadbeat father. If he chooses to be a great father, then that's great. If he chooses the deadbeat route, then you have the permission to be angry before moving on and learning from his mistakes when you are looking for a future partner.

Your father made that decision to not be a part of your life, and it is acceptable to let him know how that has affected you. Absentee fathers are not aware of the damages they cause by not being the leading man in their daughter's life, so it is okay to let him know that you needed him. If there is a reason you are not able to speak directly to your father, write a letter, or journal your thoughts. It is so important to let go of the build of aggression in order for you to move to a better place.

I once read a book entitled, "Dear Woman" by Michael E. Reid. He wrote a poem called "Daddy" for women who grew up with and without their fathers. As I read the poem, I knew he was talking to me. I found the poem's message to be deep and real. One of the best lines that was blunt but truthful read: *You can't miss something that was never there.* Can I get an Amen? When people would ask me if I was angry since my father was absent, I would just shrug my shoulders and say no before moving on to another topic. Michael took the words right out my mouth.

11. Forgive.

Forgiving is easier said than done, but in order to move forward you must forgive. I can proudly admit that I am at this point, which is why I am able to move forward with my life and accomplish all of my goals. Yes, my father does call once or twice a year and tell me he loves me, but instead of going off on why he wasn't a part of my life for the past 29 years, I just say *I love you, too*, and we hang up. I know I talked a lot about being stagnant, but not being able to forgive someone without getting an apology first is one way to keep you stuck. When you forgive, all the things I listed above will come easier, and it will make your life that much more peaceful. Once you forgive your father, you can start forgiving all of the other men that did you wrong. When I tell you I had hatred toward every man that existed, including my father, I really did, and I found it hard to be free and happy.

I was cold-hearted in some ways, because I gave up my self-esteem, my self-worth, and my dignity, and I didn't care what anyone thought. I thought I had everything under control, because I was doing things my way. Really, I was being controlled by the bitterness, the anger, the abandonment, and everything else that came along with destructive thoughts and behaviors. It wasn't until I was called into my purpose and started loving myself that I had to stop making excuses, get over the anger and bitterness, and be able to forgive, so I can give my all to the man who captured my heart. I also had to consider that if I planned on having children, how was I going to be an example for them if I couldn't model appropriate relationship skills with my own father? If you have children or plan to have children, your behaviors are very important when it comes to parenting - especially if you weren't parented properly. I encourage you to seek forgiveness with anyone who has done you wrong, even if you never get an apology. It is the only way to be free. It is the only way to be peaceful. It is the only way to break the cycle and become a better you.

Dear Dad,

I was hurt. I was broken. I was lost. I was sad. I was afraid. I hated you. I forgive you.

Your Daughter,

Ikeshia Capre

Meet the Author

Ikeshia Capre was born and raised in Canton, Ohio. She grew up in a single-parent home with her mother and her sister. She is twenty-nine years old, and she currently works for a Child Protective Services Agency. Ikeshia obtained her Bachelor's degree from Kent State University in Human Development Family Studies with a concentration in Case Management, and she is currently pursuing her master's degree in Social Work at Case Western Reserve University located in Cleveland, Ohio. Ikeshia wrote her phenomenal story to reveal how she looked for love in all the wrong places, attempted suicide as a teenager, and lived with her mother who depended on the welfare system as a primary survival source. Ikeshia hopes her story will empower women who grew up without their fathers and prevent them from becoming a product of their environment. Moreover, she hopes they will use the guide to take a step into the right direction and be the woman God called them to be.

Made in the USA
Lexington, KY
14 October 2015